D0794730

The deep freezing method of
preserving food is keyed to modern
life. With less rigid time tables, and
friends turning up unexpectedly for
meals the housewife with a stock of
food at the ready in her deep freeze
cabinet is prepared for such events
without becoming a prisoner in her
own kitchen.

Mary Norwak, herself a country
woman with a family, has written this
book with practical experience of deep
freezing food over the years. Whether
you are a beginner or more
experienced in the art you will find in
her book the answers to all the
questions you are likely to ask on the
subject.

Sphere Country Books are edited by
Barbara Hargreaves.

SPHERE COUNTRY BOOKS

June 1968   CONVERTING A COTTAGE
Suzanne Beedell

July 1968   TRAINING A DOG Sam Wilson
KEEPING A PONY Jane and Melinda
St. Clair

May 1969   WINE MAKING AND HOME
BREWING Suzanne Beedell

Deep Freezing

MARY NORWAK

SPHERE BOOKS LTD.
30/32 Gray's Inn Road, London, WC1X 8JL

First published in Great Britain in 1968
by Sphere Books
Reprinted April 1969
Reprinted October 1969
Reprinted November 1970
Reprinted June 1971
Reprinted December 1971
Reprinted October 1972
Reprinted September 1973

TRADE MARK

SPHERE

Set in Monotype Baskerville

Printed in Great Britain by
C. Nicholls & Company Ltd.

CONTENTS

INTRODUCTION

5

INTRODUCTION

There's a revolution in the kitchen as today's busy housewives discover the advantages of owning a deep freezer. 100,000 families now own a freezer, and predict a big future demand.

Instead of the cumbersome chest freezer which could only be used by country families with space and produce in abundance, or the unpredictable secondhand ice cream cabinet, there are now compact, elegant models in a range of types, sizes and prices which makes them practical for the smallest kitchen and tightest budget.

This ability to store home frozen or commercially frozen food, has given women a chance to buy according to season, and has encouraged the least domesticated to enjoy cooking and learning a new technique of preserving food.

Perhaps the happiest result of the deep-freeze revolution is that women are enjoying their kitchens again, happily experimenting with complicated dishes, batch-baking, relishing their own garden produce, and planning months ahead as their ancestors did in their still-rooms, instead of endlessly producing one-at-a-time meals in a rush.

Chapter 1

ADVANTAGES OF FREEZING

Many people who may be thinking of buying a freezer may wonder if they are going to get full value from their initial expenditure, – relatively high compared with that on other pieces of kitchen and household equipment.

The initial outlay on freezing is admittedly greater than that on bottling or canning, but this can be offset by the efficiency of a freezer and the ease with which it may be used. Freezing methods are quick and simple and leave little to chance, while bottling and canning are subject to a variety of perfect conditions not always easily achieved in an ordinary kitchen. Many women, too, have little time for the sheer labour involved in more old-fashioned methods of food preservation, and have often been discouraged by poor results.

Of particular importance to the freezer owner is the fact that certain foods such as meat, fish, poultry and game are virtually impossible to preserve by any method other than freezing. Few vegetables preserve well, and most cakes and biscuits can only be kept for a few days. But now these foods can be perfectly preserved for use weeks and months ahead in a deep freezer.

In addition to this, there are the most positive ones of saving time and money. The garden or farm can be planned to give the maximum amount of first-class produce for future use; even an unforeseen glut can be turned to advantage. But the freezer-owner of today is no longer only the farmer's wife; those in towns can take advantage of seasonal gluts at greengrocer, butcher or fishmonger to save money, yet give variety to meals months ahead.

Bulk buying gives another positive saving for the budget-conscious, not only in fresh produce but in commercially frozen food. Those with large families, or those who entertain a good deal, can use catering packs bought at budget prices, and can plan ahead for busy seasons when ready-cooked food will be a positive advantage.

For many people, the saving of time is more important than a tight budget, but as most of us know today of course time-saving can lead to money-saving. Shopping trips can waste petrol and can also be time-consuming to the housewife who may also be the family gardener or even a breadwinner too. Even the woman who has time to spare in her home will appreciate time saved for outside interests by being able to prepare a number of different meals each day by cooking in batches, making one day's cooking do the work of three of four future ones. Time taken to make an elaborate casserole for instance can be halved if a double quantity is prepared with a portion eaten on cooking day and the remainder frozen for use a week or month ahead.

Home-baking in particular takes on a new aspect when three or four cakes can be prepared at a time, perhaps to be eaten months ahead, and this enables the cook to take full advantage of time-saving electric mixers and liquidisers.

Best of all, a freezer enables a family to be well fed, on balanced meals, however busy the cook-shopper may be and whatever the weather or the price of fresh food.

BASIC RULES OF FREEZING

It is very simple to freeze food at home, but to get the full benefit of the freezer and to take out delicious food which is appetising and nourishing, certain basic rules must be observed. Some of the rules seem blindingly obvious; others will be modified as the freezer-owner gains experience and finds individual needs and ways of providing for them. Without these few rules however, end products may be less than satisfactory, while time and money will have been wasted. More specific instructions will be found in the appropriate chapters, but an initial study of the basic rules will be rewarded by a quicker grasp and greater understanding of this valuable new food preservation technique.

PLAN THE CONTENTS
Freeze food which the family enjoys and which is eaten frequently (and if possible plan the garden accordingly). Work out the type of meals the family eats, whether they enjoy pastry items, need a lot of cakes and sandwiches, enjoy and can afford roasts and grills. Work out a month's or year's budget and see where the greatest expenditure lies and whether more can be saved by freezing cheap meat in cooked dishes, home-baking cakes, or growing and freezing more fruit and vegetables. Try and work out the average monthly consumption of basic foods and see how these can best be fitted into the freezer plan in proportion to the space available. Remember that variety in menu-planning is one of the greatest benefits of a freezer.

FOLLOW THE SEASONS
Obviously home-grown fruit and vegetables will be frozen at their peak. But there are peak periods too for

produce in the shops, and constant attention should be paid to seasonal quality, wide selection and budget prices. This does not only apply to fruit and vegetables, but to dairy products and meat, poultry and game.

USE QUALITY PRODUCTS
Freezing retains high quality and good flavour, but it will not improve food. Only the best quality products are worth processing, because labour represents time and money, and freezer space and packaging are costly.

BE CLEAN
This is always an obvious rule in food preparation, but it is particularly important when preparing food for freezing. Food must be absolutely fresh, prepared in scrupulously clean utensils in a cool atmosphere, without being allowed to stand about or be contaminated by dust or insects. Packaging materials must be clean and carefully stored against future use.

WORK QUICKLY
Speed is important in retaining the freshness, flavour and nutritive value of food. Fruit and vegetables should ideally be picked and prepared within 2–3 hours. Work with only small portions at a time. Cool any blanched or cooked food quickly.

PACKAGE IN USABLE PORTIONS
Some freezer-owners need a lot of items packaged in individual one-person portions; others may need portions packed for three-or-four-portion servings; still others need bulk packs to cater for large families or staff. Assess these needs carefully before buying and preparing foods, deciding in advance when each item is most likely to be used, for what type of meal, and for how many portions.

PREPARE AND PACK FOODS PROPERLY
Follow general packaging principles (e.g. use correct

materials, seal carefully and label) and also specific instructions for each individual item. If it is found these methods do not produce satisfactory results, note this, and vary methods the next time to suit different varieties of food or individual recipes.

LABEL CAREFULLY

Indicate the type of food, the weight or number of portions, and the date of freezing. Include any special instructions for thawing, cooking or seasoning. If packing fruit or vegetables, include the name of each variety and compare results for future freezer planning.

ORGANISE SPACE

Some people like to keep certain types of food together, and this certainly makes it easier to assess supplies. An orderly freezer holds more food and saves time in finding packages. Food to be used first should be most accessible.

KEEP AN INVENTORY

An inventory helps in planning for the freezer for each successive season, indicating those foods which are eaten constantly and those which are neglected. A list of food reminds the freezer-user to keep a constant turnover of items; it also serves in menu planning giving a quick reference guide to the food available. Each person will evolve an individual method, but necessary details are the type of food, the number of packages, the date of freezing and the number of packages already removed.

USE THE FREEZER CONSTANTLY

The freezer is not a miser's hoard. Using food, not saving it indefinitely, pays dividends in time, work and money. Empty space is using up electricity, so keep the freezer well filled with a variety of food which is used daily. Don't plan to carry food over from one season to the next, and use *first* the food which has been frozen *longest*.

NEVER REFREEZE

An obvious rule which is neglected at the freezer-owner's peril. Therefore pack in usable portions and only take out those items which will be cooked and eaten immediately. Thawed items will keep in the refrigerator for a short time, but must never be returned to the freezer.

Chapter 3

BUYING A FREEZER

The two main considerations in buying a freezer must obviously be price and storage capacity, but a number of secondary considerations such as running costs, likely use and positioning in the home must affect final choice.

Not long ago the potential buyer had more or less to put up with a chest-type freezer designed only for function and not appearance. Since most freezer-buyers were country housewives with outbuildings or large kitchens where a freezer could be placed, the consideration of poor appearance or sheer bulk did not affect choice. Those who could not afford this type of freezer made do with a used model which had stored commercial frozen food or conserved ice cream, and these lent even less attraction to the domestic scene.

Now the deep freeze revolution has spread to all types of home, to town and country households, to those with small modern kitchens and little space to spare. As a result, the manufacturers are producing three main types of freezer which not only suit a variety of budgets and storage needs, but which also look good in the home: the chest, the upright and the freezer/refrigerator in an enormous range of sizes. Before deciding which of the three types suits individual needs, it is best to assess the general needs of all freezer owners.

SPACE AVAILABLE

While the owner of a small kitchen will have little choice in the positioning of a freezer, those with more space should think carefully about the placing of the machine. The ideal place for a freezer should be dry, cool and well ventilated.

Dampness can damage both the exterior and the motor, and if a freezer is put into a garage or outhouse, a basement or larder, this must be a first consideration.

Excessive heat will make the motor work harder to maintain the low temperature constantly required in the freezer. If a freezer must be in a kitchen, it should be as far as possible from any heat source.

Air must circulate freely round the freezer so that heat will be efficiently removed from the condenser and freezers should not be fitted closely into cupboard spaces.

LIKELY USE

It may seem a small point, but it is important to assess the likely daily use of a freezer. A farm freezer may perhaps be mainly used to keep bulk supplies of vegetables and poultry, so that infrequent use is likely, and a short walk to the freezer will affect nobody. The same freezer however, filled with cakes and cooked meals and used two or three times a day, will become an irritant if it adds up to yet more journeys for the user. Thus the much-used freezer should be very easily accessible.

STORAGE CAPACITY

The storage space needed will depend on family size, on entertaining, and on whether much home produce is to be stored. Maximum storage space is calculated by multiplying each cubic foot by 30 to give storage capacity in pounds per cubic foot. In actual fact, this figure will be somewhat reduced in practice, since there will be many irregularly shaped packages, and lightweight packs which take up more space. 1 cubic foot of space holds about 16 1 pint cartons or 20 pounds meat or poultry or 35 square or rectangular 1 pint cartons.

As when buying most domestic equipment, it is better to over-estimate family needs, since too small a freezer soon becomes irritating, and it is always difficult to sell electrical equipment secondhand.

COST OF RUNNING

Basic electricity charges are not the only thing which affects the running cost of a freezer. The size of the machine and its design, the number of times it is opened and the length of time, and whether the food is thoroughly chilled before being put inside. The manufacturer will give an estimate of current likely to be used by individual machines. As a rough guide, a 6 cubic foot freezer uses .3 kw per cubic foot per 24 hours; 12 cubic foot uses .25 kw per cubic ft; 18 cubic foot uses .20 kw per cubic foot.

BUYING A USED FREEZER

There was a time when buying a used freezer which had come from shop or factory after conserving frozen food or ice cream was worthwhile for the family on a limited budget, since many of these were available for about £20. However, there were always problems of maintainance, with seldom a guarantee available and possibly expensive repairs. Now that manufacturers have produced small domestic freezers, well designed and at competitive prices with fair guarantees and an availability of spare parts, it is rarely worth buying a used commercial freezer.

Once the basic essentials are assessed, it is time to decide between the relative merits of the three types of freezer.

CHEST FREEZERS

This type of freezer is very suitable for storage in an outhouse or garage. Smaller sizes (4 and 6.2 cubic foot) are now available and very suitable for kitchen use, often providing an extra working surface. The very large chests qualify as commercial freezers and are free of tax, so these are often a better buy than the large domestic freezer.

When choosing a chest freezer, see that all items will be easily accessible to the user, as packages at the bottom and back of the freezer can be difficult to reach. For this reason, look for a freezer fitted with dividers so that food may be more easily arranged and also see if baskets are provided. If they are, check the weight of a basket filled with food to see if it is within the user's lifting capacity.

Be sure to check that there is a magnetic lid seal, and a self-balancing lid to make food removal easier and safer. If the freezer is to be stored some way from the house in a garage or outhouse, it is sense to buy one with a lock. Additional refinements may be interior lights and a warning light or bell for power failure.

UPRIGHT FREEZERS

The upright freezer is generally more attractive in a kitchen, and has the advantage of easy access and quicker visual checks on food supplies. One important consideration is that upright freezers have their weight concentrated in a small area, and it is wise to see that floors will take this weight. It used to be said that there was a greater loss of cold air from the opening of an upright rather than a chest freezer, but this is in fact negligible.

When buying an upright freezer, look for high capacity shelves in doors and a good door seal. Once again, check whether a short person can reach the back of upper shelves. Look for useful extras like interior lights and warning systems. One or two upright freezers contain special freezer shelves for quick freezing, which are particularly valuable for those who will be freezing their own vegetables and are able by fast freezing to use the loose-pack method which saves packing space and is more convenient when large packages are to be divided for use.

FREEZER-REFRIGERATORS

This is the latest development in freezer design and for the town housewife or the one with a small kitchen, it provides the most practical and attractive answer to the space problem.

In it's simplest form, the freezer is designed as a small independent unit of about 1·75 cubic foot capacity which can be placed on a shelf or in a larder or, better still, formed into a unit with a matching refrigerator from the same manufacturer. The storage capacity of these small freezers is obviously fairly limited, but will hold about 60 pounds of frozen food, which can represent a reasonable amount of commercial products together with one or two prepared meals, cakes, or special meat or poultry.

Those who need a larger freezer but still have little floor space will appreciate the specially designed refrigerator-freezers which are in effect freezers on top of refrigerators with dual controls. These come in large sizes, but due consideration must be given to the headroom needed and to floor strength. A particular attraction of these combined machines is that the refrigerator normally has an automatic defrosting device, which saves yet another kitchen chore.

FREEZER MANUFACTURERS

It is obviously impossible to discuss current designs and prices since in a rapidly expanding market, manufacturers are developing new freezers very quickly. The following manufacturers each make a variety of domestic and commercial freezers, and brochures may be obtained from local Electricity Service Centres or direct from the manufacturer. Occasionally large shop-soiled models from well-known manufacturers are available at considerable reductions from large stores, and are worth looking at.

ENGLISH ELECTRIC LTD., English Electric House, Strand, London W.C.2.

HELIMATIC LTD. (Electrolux), Airport House, Purley Way, Croydon, Surrey.

HOOVER LTD., Perivale, Greenford, Middx.

KELVINATOR LTD., Chiswick Flyover, Great West Road, London W.4.

PHILLIPS ELECTRICAL LTD., Century House, Shaftesbury Avenue, London W.C.2.

PRESTCOLD Division of Pressed Steel Co. Ltd., Theale, Reading, Berks.

TOTAL REFRIGERATION LTD., 46 Gorst Road, London, N.W.10.

Chapter 4

FREEZER CARE

Like all modern electrical equipment, a freezer is designed to be used with ease and efficiency by the housewife with very little regular maintainance. The manufacturer will see that the machine is correctly installed and tested, and controls will be regulated.

After initial installation and testing, the freezer must be prepared for use, and from then on will run with little attention externally and internally. Each manufacturer issues a booklet which gives details of basic maintainance and of food preparation for the freezer, and the local electricity showroom or manufacturer can be consulted if problems arise. Home economists can be contacted through local showrooms to give advice on individual appliances and food preparation problems.

PREPARING THE FREEZER
After installation and testing, the freezer should be turned off, and washed inside with plain warm water, then dried thoroughly. During this process, the thermostat control knob should not be adjusted as it will be pre-set to the temperature required. If a control knob gives variable settings, as in freezer-refrigerators, it should be set, after cleaning, at the recommended temperature for everyday use. When the freezer is switched on again, it should be left for 12 hours before use, so that the cabinet is thoroughly chilled.

CLEANING THE FREEZER
The outside of the machine should be cleaned with warm soapy water, when necessary, and polished with an enamel surface polish according to the manufacturer's specific instructions.

The inside of the machine should be cleaned after

defrosting according to manufacturer's instructions. If in doubt, use a solution of 1 tablespoon bicarbonate of soda to 1 quart water which is just warm. Rinse with clean water and dry thoroughly. Do not use soap, detergent or caustic cleaners.

DEFROSTING

Some freezers defrost automatically and only need the drain emptying. Frost does not seriously affect food storage unless it is very thick, and defrosting once or twice a year should be sufficient if this is to be done manually. Normally a freezer should be defrosted when ice is $\frac{1}{4}$ inch thick, and it is best to defrost when stocks of food are low.

Take the food from the freezer and pack it closely in a refrigerator or wrap in layers of newspaper and blankets and put into a cold place. Line the bottom of the freezer with paper to catch frost scrapings, turn off current, and scrape frost with a plastic or wooden spatula. *Do not scrape with sharp tools or wire brushes.*

If it is not contrary to manufacturer's instructions, vessels of warm water may be put into the chest while leaving the door or lid open, but hot water must not touch the cold surfaces. Cold water may be used to speed melting ice.

After defrosting, wipe and dry the freezer completely Switch on to coldest setting, run machine for 30 minutes, then replace packages. After 3 hours, return switch to normal everyday setting.

POWER FAILURE

Some freezers are fitted with a warning device which will ring a bell or show a light when power fails. If there is a warning signal, first check the machine has not been switched off by mistake. Check fuses. If these are in order and the power failure is general, report to the Electricity Service Centre. Do not attempt to touch the freezer motor.

Food in the freezer will last about 12 hours safely in the

event of power failure, but this will depend on the load of food and on insulation.

Food lasts better if the freezer is full of frozen packets. If the power failure is likely to be only a short one, avoid opening the door or lid unless absolutely necessary.

Chapter 5

BASIC EQUIPMENT AND
PACKAGING MATERIALS

The initial outlay on packaging material for the freezer
may seem high, but without the correct wrapping,
expensive food will deteriorate and will lose colour,
flavour and nutritive value (see Chapter 7 "What Goes
Wrong, and Why"). Food must be protected against
drying out, against the presence of air which will cause
deterioration, and against crossing of smells and
flavours.

In addition packaging material must be easy to handle,
and must not be liable to split, burst or leak, and must
withstand the low temperature at which the freezer is
maintained. The essentials of good packaging materials
must therefore be: 1. moisture-vapour-proof; 2. waterproof; 3. greaseproof; 4. smell-free; 5. durable; 6. easily
handled; 7. economically stored; 8. resistant to low
temperatures.

Many ordinary packing materials such as greaseproof
and transparent papers and lightweight foils will not
answer all these conditions. It is important therefore to
buy only such materials as have been tested and proved
satisfactory in the freezer. It is possible, however, to use
certain containers which are in everyday use, such as
plastic boxes and glass jars if they fulfil the necessary
conditions.

WAXED TUBS
These round waxed tubs are particularly suitable for
freezing fruit in syrup, and are also useful for soups and
purees. Available in a variety of sizes, holding from 8
fluid ounces to 80 fluid ounces they have flush airtight
lids, and additional lids can be supplied for re-use. Extra
strong tubs with screw-tops are also available in a number

of sizes, and cream tubs ranging from $2\frac{1}{2}$ fluid ounces to 20 fluid ounces sizes can be bought, together with spare lids. Tubs should only be filled to within $\frac{3}{4}$ inch of the lid when closed.

WAXED CARTONS WITH FITTED LIDS
Rectangular boxes with lids which must be sealed with special freezer tape are available in 1 pound and 2 pound sizes and are suitable for asparagus and other vegetables, carved meats, sliced fruits.

WAXED BOXES WITH TUCK-IN LIDS
These are tall containers which can be useful when space is limited, and they come in $\frac{1}{2}$ pint, 1 pint and 2 pint sizes. They can be used for soups, purees, fruit in syrup and vegetables, and must be sealed with special freezer tape.

WAXED CARTONS WITH LINERS
It is recommended that some foods particularly subject to leakage be packed in waxed cartons with polythene liners. These are available in 2 pint size, and only the liners need be sealed.

RIGID PLASTIC BOXES
Transparent boxes with close-fitting lids which can be used indefinitely, and are extremely useful for frozen items which may be carried while thawing such as sandwiches or fruit for lunches. They are also useful for items like stews which can be turned out into a saucepan for thawing, as the flexible sides can be lightly pressed to aid removal. For long term storage, the lid should be sealed with special deep-freeze tape, but it is important that the boxes have perfectly fitting air tight lids. There are now available special Swedish freezer boxes which can be boiled for sterilization, and which are made to stack and save space, but most branded plastic boxes are suitable for freezer storage.

GLASS JARS

Screw top preserving jars, bottles and honey jars may be used for freezing if they have been tested first for resistance to low temperatures. To do this, put an empty jar into a plastic bag and put into freezer overnight; if the jar breaks, the bag will hold the pieces. These jars are easy to use and economical in storage space, but $\frac{1}{2}$ to 1 inch headspace must be allowed for expansion which might cause breakage. Jars are very useful for soups and stews, but be careful not to use those with "shoulders" which make thawing difficult if the items are needed in a hurry.

POLYTHENE SHEETS

These sheets are useful for wrapping joints, poultry and large pies, and pieces of sheeting may be used to divide meat, etc. for easy thawing. The wrapper must be sealed with special deep-freeze tape.

POLYTHENE BAGS

These bags are very cheap to use and simple to handle. They may be used for meat, poultry, fruit and vegetables, pies, cakes and sandwiches. Buy bags which are gusseted for easy packing. They may be sealed by heat or twist fastening (see Chapter 6 "Packing for the Freezer"). If the bags are subject to frequent handling, they should be overwrapped to avoid punctures. If the contents are likely to contaminate other items with their smell and flavour, they should also be overwrapped. It is most important to see that air is excluded from polythene bags (see Chapter 6 "Packing for the Freezer", and photographic section, for the best method of doing this).

FREEZER PAPER

This type of specially treated paper has been popular for a long time in America and Canada, but is only just coming into use here. 50 foot rolls of paper 18 inches wide are packaged in a dispensing box with metal tearing edge. The paper is strong and does not puncture easily, is moisture-vapour-proof without becoming brittle, is highly resistant to fats and grease and strips off easily when food is frozen or thawed. The paper is specially coated inside and has an uncoated outer surface on which labelling details may be written.

FOIL
Foil dishes are very useful for freezing cooked food. They include a variety of pie and pudding dishes, patty pans, and compartment trays for freezing whole meals with a variety of ingredients. The food is normally cooked in the dishes, then packed into polythene or freezer paper for freezing. It is sometimes useful to pack individual items such as baked apples or meat patties into foil trays, then polythene, for easy handling.

FASTENING MATERIALS
Sealing materials are most important to complete packaging.

Politape is a special deep-freeze sealing tape, 1 inch wide, and its gum is resistant to low temperatures so that it will not loosen and curl. This is available in 36 yard rolls.

Bambo is a sealing unit for welding polythene seams on bags and sheeting, though this can be done with a domestic iron.

Tite-Tie Bag Fasteners can be used on polythene bags instead of heat sealing to give a simple air-tight closure.

OVERWRAPPING
When packages are subject to heavy handling and possible puncture, or when there is danger of cross-flavours, they can be overwrapped with ordinary brown paper, or with stockinette (mutton cloth).

SHEET WRAPPINGS
Sheet wrappings other than polythene include heat-sealing Cellophane, and heavy-duty foil. Owing to the danger of puncturing, it is advisable to overwrap. Foil

has the advantage that it can be used for reheating food direct from the freezer. "Saran" wrap, a very pliable transparent wrapping, has been in use for some time in America, and is now available over here. Pliability is the advantage of these three types of wrapping, which ensures a tight package and elimination of air.

All packaging materials may be obtained from Frigicold Ltd., 10 Manchester Square, London, W.1., who will supply a variety of Basic Freezer Packs for the new freezer-owner. A comprehensive illustrated catalogue and price list is available on application.

It is important that packaging materials should be stored carefully. They should be stacked in a dry, pestproof place, preferably packed in polythene to exclude dust. Most items may be washed, dried and stored in sterile condition for future use. Hot water should not be used for washing. Bags and boxes to be re-used should be carefully examined for punctures, tears or fractures.

EXTRA EQUIPMENT

One or two supplementary items are needed for deep-freezing in addition to packaging materials. Most of these will be already available in the kitchen.

1. A fine-mesh wire basket with handle for blanching. If a special blancher is not available, a fine-meshed deep-frying basket, a salad shaker or a cheesecloth bag can be used.

2. A saucepan or steamer with lid, large enough to hold blancher.

3. Labelling items. Waxed or "felt" pencils must be used to avoid fading. Labels with special freezer-proof gum should be used for packages which cannot be written upon, or paper may be inserted in the packages.

4. Normal kitchen equipment which will be needed for food preparation for the freezer includes (a) a bowl for immersing blancher (b) a sharp knife (c) a funnel for filling bags.

Chapter 6

PACKING FOR THE FREEZER

The importance of correct packaging for the freezer cannot be overstressed, because of its great influence on the end-product. Once the food has been correctly prepared, and the correct packaging chosen, the two must be perfectly combined to give successful results. The aim of packaging for the freezer is to eliminate air at the beginning, then to exclude air during storage. In this book, individual wrappings and packing methods are given for each food item or recipe. This chapter concerns the general principles of packaging for success.

PRELIMINARY WRAPPING

All food should be prepared in the way in which it will be most useful when it is taken from the freezer e.g. meat cut and trimmed; poultry trussed. Before beginning the freezing process, all packaging materials should be assembled, any special tools required should be laid out, and the food completely prepared.

Meat should be prepared with sheets of Cellophane or greaseproof paper to separate slices; bones or protrubances on meat or poultry should be covered with a padding of paper; cakes without icing should be layered with separating paper.

SHEET WRAPPING

Food to be wrapped should be in the centre of the sheet of packaging material. Draw two sides of the sheet together above the fold and fold them neatly downwards over the food to bring the wrapping as close to the food as possible. Seal this fold, then fold ends like a parcel to make them close and tight, excluding air. Seal all folds. Overwrap if necessary.

BAG WRAPPING

See that bags are completely open before filling. If using liquid or semi-liquid food, make sure it goes down into corners and leaves no air pockets. Use a funnel to avoid a mess at the top of the bag. Seal with a heat or twist closing. To make packages easier to handle and store, bags can be placed in other rigid containers for filling and freezing, then removed in a more compact form.

CARTONS AND RIGID CONTAINERS

Moisture will expand during freezing, so headspace must be left between the surface of the food and the seal of the container. Usually ½ inch space is left for most foods; ½ to 1 inch headspace is necessary for liquids according to the size of the container (see individual packaging directions). Some foods, such as fruit in syrup, will rise to the surface and may discolour. They should be covered with a piece of Cellophane pressed into the surface of the liquid, and space above can be filled with more crumpled Cellophane.

EXCLUDING AIR

It is most important to exclude air and to remove air pockets in packages. Most simply this is done by pressing the package with the hands. Air pockets in cartons can be released by plunging a knife into the contents two or three times.

The most satisfactory way of removing air from bags is to insert a drinking straw, hold the closing tightly, and suck out air until the package holds close to the food (see photograph).

LOOSE PACKING

This system of freezing is very useful for items such as peas and raspberries, which are frozen individually, then poured into a container. Frozen by this method, a small number can be shaken out for use without the necessity of chopping up a frozen block or thawing a large quantity. This method can be achieved by freezing the fruit or vegetables uncovered on a baking sheet on the floor of the freezer before putting them into containers or bags with no headspace. The newest freezer-refrigerators have a special freezer shelf for this type of fast-freezing.

SEALING
All packages must be sealed by one of three methods.
(a) *Taping*. Special freezer-proof tape must be used, and should be on containers with lids, and on sheet-wrapped items. Be sure that all folds are taped.
(b) *Heat*. Polythene bags may be sealed by a special type of iron, but a domestic iron can be used successfully if a piece of paper is put between the iron and the polythene to be fused. Heat-sealing gives a neat package which can be stored easily.
(c) *Twist-tying*. After extracting air from polythene bag, a plastic-covered fastener should be twisted round the end of the bag, the top of the bag turned down over this twist, and the fastener twisted again round the bunched neck of the bag.

LABELLING
All items in a freezer should be clearly labelled with contents, weight or number of portions, date of freezing, and any special thawing, heating or seasoning instructions. A waxed or "felt" pencil must be used as ordinary ink and lead fade at low temperatures. Ordinary gummed labels will curl and drop off at low temperatures, so use special labels, tuck a label into a transparent package, or write directly on the freezer wrap.

FREEZING
Packages to be frozen should be placed in the coldest part of the freezer, as recommended by the manufacturer, and are normally frozen in contact with a refrigerated surface. Manufacturers' instructions will indicate any special temperature control which may be

necessary, the amount which can be frozen at any one time, and the length of time for which the package should remain in freezing position before being moved to storage position.

When arranging food in storage, it may be divided into food types e.g. meat, fish, cooked dishes. More practically, it can be stored in three categories; (a) food for current consumption to be easily accessible; (b) food to be stored for a length of time ;(c) seasonal food such as fruit which should be eaten in rotation so that items are not still in the freezer when a new season comes round.

KEEPING RECORDS
It is most important to keep records to know where food has been placed and how much has been used. A ready check on storage times is also provided if there is an indication of a date by which an item should be taken out and used. A suggested record sheet shows how items are deleted as used.

Position	Item	Size of Pack	Number	Date	To be used by
Shelf B	Raspberries	½ pound	4 3 2	8/6/68	1/4/69
Shelf B	Raspberries	2 pounds	3 2 1	8/6/68	1/4/69
Shelf C	Pheasant		2	6/11/68	1/6/69
Shelf C	Chicken Casserole	4 portions	2 1	1/7/68	1/8/68

Chapter 7

WHAT GOES WRONG AND WHY

Mistakes in the freezer are costly in view of the price of food and packaging materials, and a loss of colour, flavour and nutritive value should be avoided. Providing the freezer is functioning well at storage temperature and the food has been processed correctly, all problems come back to the basic one of good packaging materials and careful wrapping.

It is extremely important that food should be quick-frozen to retard enzymic action. An enzyme is a type of protein in food which accelerates chemical reactions, but the freezing process slows down the reactions which encourage the reproduction of harmful bacteria. The enzymic action in vegetables is relatively slow in vegetables compared with animal products and cooked foods, and the quicker food is frozen the safer it will be from harmful reactions.

Likewise, of course, food should be eaten or cooked immediately after thawing, for the thawing process hurries up enzymic action and encourages more rapid deterioration. Basically then, there are four main points to bear in mind when dealing with frozen food to ensure perfect results:

1. Prepare and freeze food quickly.
2. Do not freeze more food at any one time than is recommended by the manufacturer of the freezer.
3. Use correct wrappings, perfectly sealed.
4. Thaw and cook food quickly.

Assuming food is quickly prepared, packaging is the point at which things are likely to go wrong. The freezer is designed as a box of cold dry air. Moisture contains heat until it reaches the solidifying or freezing stage. When a package is put into a freezer, a battle ensues

32

between the heat in that package and the surrounding cold dry air. The cold air attempts to draw out the warmth and moisture from the food. Warmth must be withdrawn to produce the freezing process, but if moisture goes out too, the result is disastrous, and is called dehydration.

DEHYDRATION

Dehydration is the removal of moisture and juices from food, and may not occur immediately, but after a long period of storage. Meat is particularly subject to this problem, giving a tough, dry and tasteless result. It can only be avoided by careful wrapping in moisture-vapour-proof packaging. A side-effect of dehydration is the unpleasant condition known as "freezer burn" (see note).

OXIDATION

Oxidation is a process whereby oxygen moves inwards from air to food, so that food must be protected by an oxygen barrier i.e. the correct wrappings. The effect of oxidation is to cause the mingling of oxygen with food fat cells, which react to form chemicals which give meat and fish a bad taste and smell, and fatty foods are particularly liable to this problem (see rancidity).

FREEZER BURN

This is the effect of dehydration which causes discoloured greyish-brown areas on the surface of food when it is removed from the freezer. It is only avoided by correct packaging materials, wrapping and sealing.

RANCIDITY

This is the effect of oxidation or absorbtion of oxygen into fat cells, and is recognised by the unpleasant flavour and smell of the food affected. Fried foods suffer from this problem, and are not generally recommended for freezer storage. Salt accelerates the reaction which causes rancidity and should not be added to minced meat or sausages before freezing; salt butter will have a shorter freezer life than fresh butter.

Pork is particularly subject to rancidity, since it contains not only thick layers of fat but also has a greater number of tiny fat cells than other meat, so that its freezer life is shorter. Pork and fat fish, which has similar problems, should be fast-frozen.

BROKEN PACKAGES
A package which is suffering from dehydration or oxidation may have been broken. Rough handling, sharp edges in packages, brittleness of wrapping, or a too-full container can cause cracks. Thus all wrappings should be strong, and sheet wrappings should be so pliable that they can be closely moulded to the food. Coated sheet wrappings are subject to internal cracking if they are pierced by the contents or become brittle at low temperatures, and only tested materials should be used.

CROSS-FLAVOURING
Strongly-flavoured foods may affect other items in storage with their smell or flavour and should be carefully overwrapped.

FLABBINESS
Fruit and vegetables which are flabby and limp may be of the wrong variety for freezing, and this must be subject to trial and error. In general, however, depending on cell structure, slow-freezing of fruit and vegetables will result in flabbiness.

ICE CRYSTALS
Too great headspace on top of liquid foods such as soup may cause a layer of ice crystals to form which will affect storage and flavour. This is not too serious in liquids which will be heated or thawed, as the liquid melts back into its original form and can be shaken or stirred back into emulsion.

However, meat, fish, vegetables and fruit can be

affected by ice crystals if slow-freezing has taken place. Moisture in the food cells forms ice which will expand if slow-frozen, and in occupying more space these crystals will puncture and destroy surrounding tissues. This breaking down of tissues allows juices, particularly in meat, to escape, taking with them flavour.

Chapter 8

STORAGE TIMES

There is no hard and fast rule for determining storage times for food stored in the freezer. The type of food and the care taken in preparation, packaging and freezing will affect final results. It is often possible to keep food longer than the "rule" allows, but this is usually only discovered because the food in question has been tucked away and forgotten.

Uncooked i.e. raw food will keep longer than anything cooked. Salt will shorten storage life, and seasonings will develop off-flavours, which while not dangerous will certainly be unpleasant. Bad packing, leaving air spaces, and the wrong type of packaging material (that which is not moisture-vapour-proof) will also affect the keeping qualities of frozen food (see Chapter 7 "What Goes Wrong and Why").

The following chart gives reasonable maximum safe storage times, but individual freezing instructions and recipes give a specific time for storage throughout the book. When in doubt, it is better to aim at a short storage period. Certainly with cooked foods, a rapid turnover is ideal, and a month is the storage maximum to aim at.

STORAGE TIME CHART

Item	Maximum Safe Storage (Months)
MEAT	
Beef, lamb, pork, veal (all fresh and unsalted)	8 – 12
Beef, minced (unsalted)	9
Sausages	1
Offal	2 – 3
Ham and Bacon (whole)	3 – 4

Ham and Bacon (sliced)	2 weeks
POULTRY	6 – 8
GAME	6 – 8
FISH	
Fat (mackerel, herring, salmon)	2 – 3
Lean white (cod, plaice, sole)	6
Shellfish	1
DAIRY PRODUCTS	
Butter	4 – 6
Cheese	4 – 5
Cream	3 – 4
Eggs	8 – 12
FRUIT	8 – 12
FRUIT JUICES	8 – 12
VEGETABLES	8 – 12
YEAST BREAD, ROLLS AND BUNS	
Baked	8 – 12
Unbaked	2
BISCUITS	
Unbaked	4 – 6
CAKES	
Baked	3 – 4
Unbaked	1
PIES	
Baked	6
Unbaked	1 – 2
COOKED DISHES	1

Chapter 9

MEAT

Fresh and cooked meat store excellently in the freezer and represent a great saving of money and time if shopping and preparation are carefully planned. A freezer enables the housewife to buy some cuts of meat when prices are low, or to buy in bulk, and to prepare in advance complicated meat dishes or those which require a long time in the oven.

It is a temptation to take advantage of bulk buying, but the value of this must be carefully assessed. If a lamb is purchased for instance, the cost of the leg, shoulder and loin meat will be reduced, but there will be a quantity of incidental cuts such as breasts, neck and offal which may not be to individual family taste, may take up valuable freezer room, or may take too long to prepare for the busy or inexperienced cook. If high quality roasts and quick-cooking steaks or chops are desired, and cost is not too important, it can be worth purchasing these in bulk; some shops make seasonal offers of this type of meat for freezing. Where money must be more thoughtfully spent but time is still limited and simply-cooked meats such as roasts and chops are more useful than casseroles, it is worth buying frozen imported meat at low seasonal prices, if it is transferred direct from the butcher's store room to the home freezer with no interim thawing period. (For fuller details of bulk purchases, see Chapter 27 "Buying in Bulk".)

It is very important, however, not to overload the freezer with bulky quantities of meat, and also to keep a good regular turnover of supplies. The best compromise is to use the freezer for keeping special high quality cuts or those which are not often obtainable such as pork fillet, veal and fillet steak, together with a variety of prepared dishes made from the cheaper cuts which are useful for future occasions when time is short for food preparation.

However the individual choice is made, it is important to remember that the freezer will not improve the quality of meat. Tender meat can become a little more tender in storage, but nothing will improve texture or flavour of poor meat.

PREPARATION FOR FREEZING

Good quality meat should be chosen, and hung for the required time. Meat should be packaged in quantities suitable for use on one occasion. If possible, meat should be boned and surplus fat removed so as not to take up unnecessary freezer space; if bones are not removed, ends should be wrapped in several layers of greaseproof paper to avoid piercing freezer wrapping. Meat should be packed in polythene for easy identification, and labelling is very important as with all freezer items. It is most important to exclude air from packages so that the freezer wrap stays close to surface of meat (see Chapter 7 "How to Pack for Freezing"). If a whole animal or a variety of different meats are being prepared for freezing at one time, begin with the offal, then pork, then veal and lamb, and finally beef as this will keep best under refrigeration if delays occur. Normally, no more than 4 pounds of meat per cubic foot of freezer space should be frozen at one time for best results.

It is important that wrapping for meat should be strong, since oxygen from the air which may penetrate wrappings affects fat and causes rancidity (pork is of course most subject to this problem). In addition to moisture-vapour-proof wrapping, an overwrap of brown paper, greaseproof paper or stockinette will protect packages and will guard against punctures from projecting bones or other packets. It is worth taking this precaution, since meat is likely to be the most costly item stored in the freezer.

JOINTS

Joints of beef, lamb, mutton, pork or veal should be prepared in the form in which they will be cooked for the table i.e. bones removed if necessary, surplus fat trimmed, and meat tied into shape. Wipe meat with a cloth and pad any sharp bones with several layers of greaseproof paper. Wrap and seal in moisture-vapour-proof packing, excluding as much air as possible, over-wrap and label. Storage times: Beef 10–12 months; lamb, mutton and veal 6–8 months; pork 4 months.

STEAKS AND CHOPS

Package in quantities most likely to be needed at one time. Put a sheet of Cellophane or greaseproof paper between pieces of meat for easy separation. Pack compactly in parcel pack or polythene bag. For easy storage, each piece of meat can be wrapped separately and stored in quantities in polythene bags, so individual portions may be removed.

PREPARED MEATS

A lot of time can be saved if cut-up fresh meat is frozen for use in casseroles, and if mince is packed in quantities, or in the form of hamburgers. Stewing steak should be trimmed of fat, cut into cubes and pressed down compactly into containers. Mince should be of good quality, without much fat, and packed tightly into bags or cartons to exclude air. No salt should be added as this reduces storage life. Shaped patties of meat for hamburgers take less time to thaw than a bulk package of meat, so these can be shaped, separated by a sheet of Cellophane or greaseproof paper, and packed into bags or cartons. Storage time: 2 months.

OFFAL

Hearts, liver, kidneys, sweetbreads and tongue can all be frozen. They should be washed thoroughly, blood vessels and pipes removed, and dried. Wrap each item in Cellophane or polythene, and put into cartons or bags.

Liver may be frozen whole or sliced, and if sliced should be divided with Cellophane or greaseproof paper for easy separation. Storage time: 3 months. Tripe, cut in 1 inch cubes, may be stored for 2 months.

SAUSAGES
If home-made sausages are prepared, omit salt as this shortens freezer life by speeding up rancidity in frozen fat. Sausage meat or sausages should be wrapped in moisture-vapour-proof wrapping. Storage time: 1 month.

THAWING FROZEN MEAT
Frozen meat may be cooked thawed or unthawed, but partial or complete thawing helps retain juiciness, and this is the best method to follow. Thin cuts of meat and minced meat may toughen if cooked from the frozen state. Offal must always be completely thawed. Meat is best thawed in its wrapping, and preferably in a refrigerator since slow even thawing is required. Allow 5 hours per pound in a refrigerator and 2 hours per pound at room temperature. If it is really necessary to hurry thawing, this can be done in a cool oven (200°F or Gas Mark ½) allowing 25 minutes per pound, but flavour will not be so good. If meat must be cooked from the frozen state, unthawed large cuts will take 1½ times as long as fresh ones; smaller thin cuts will take 1¼ times as long. When thawing offal, sausages and mince, allow 1½ hours at room temperature or 3 hours in a refrigerator.

COOKING FROZEN MEAT
Meat which has been frozen may be roast, braised, grilled, fried or stewed in the same way as fresh meat. In any roasting process, however, it is best to use a slow oven method (for beef, use 300°F or Gas Mark 2, and also for lamb; for pork use 350°F. or Gas Mark 4). Frozen chops and steaks will cook well if put into a thick frying pan just rubbed with fat and cooked very gently for the first 5 minutes on each side, then browned more

quickly. Meat should be cooked as soon as it is thawed, and still cold, to prevent loss of juices.

HAM AND BACON

Cured and smoked meats are best stored in a cool atmosphere, protected from flies and dust, and there is no advantage in freezing them. They may of course be frozen, and are then better in the piece rather than slices, but storage time is limited to 3–4 months. Meat stored in this way should be overwrapped. Sliced bacon may for convenience be stored in the freezer, wrapped in moisture-vapour-proof wrapping, but storage time is limited to 3 weeks.

COOKED MEAT DISHES

There can be great time-saving in freezing prepared meat dishes to eat cold, and to reheat for serving. There is little advantage in pre-cooking joints, steaks or chops, since the outer surface sometimes develops an off-flavour, and reheating will dry out the meat. Cold meat from joints can of course be frozen in slices with or without sauce. Fried meats tend to toughness, dryness and rancidity when frozen. Any combination dishes of meat and vegetables should include the vegetables when they are slightly undercooked to avoid softness on reheating. It is very important that all cooked meats should be cooled quickly for freezing.

SLICED COLD MEAT

Joints of meat may be sliced and frozen to serve cold. Slices should be at least ¼ inch thick, separated by Cellophane or greaseproof paper, and packed tightly together to avoid drying out of surfaces, then put into cartons or bags. Meat slices should be thawed for 3 hours in a refrigerator in the container, then separated and spread on absorbent paper to remove moisture. Ham and pork lose colour when stored in this way. Storage time: 2 months.

Sliced cold meat may also be packaged with a good

gravy, thickened with cornflour. Both meat and gravy must be cooled quickly before packing. The slices in gravy are easiest to handle if packed in foil dishes, then in bags, as the frozen dish may be put straight into the oven in the foil for reheating; if the foil dish is covered with foil before being packaged, this foil lid will help to keep the meat moist in reheating. Heat the frozen dish at 350°F. (Gas Mark 4) for 25 minutes. Storage time: 1 month.

GALANTINES AND MEAT LOAVES
Galantines and meat loaves made with minced meat are very useful to keep in the refrigerator, particularly when school holidays or the picnic season are in the offing. They are most easily stored if prepared in loaf tins for cooking, then turned-out, wrapped and frozen. Meat loaves may be frozen uncooked, and this is most easily achieved if the mixture is packed into loaf tins lined with foil, the foil then being formed into a parcel and put into the freezer; the frozen meat can then be transferred to its original tin for baking. For quick serving, meat loaves and galantines may be packed in slices. Pack slices with a piece of Cellophane or greaseproof paper between each, reform loaf shape and pack for freezing. Slices can be separated while still frozen, and thawed quickly on absorbent paper. Storage time: 1 month.

CASSEROLES AND STEWS
Meat freezes well in sauces, provided there is enough liquid to cover the meat completely and prevent drying out. Vegetables should if possible be slightly under-cooked to avoid softness. Potatoes, rice and other starch additions should be kept to the minimum as they do not freeze well in liquid and will be soft, with a tendency to off-flavours. Cornflour should be used rather than ordinary flavour to prevent curdling, and sauces and gravies will tend to thicken slightly in storage. With these small reservations, any favourite recipe may be used,

43

including those which contain wine, but keeping the fat content as low as possible.

For easy packing and reheating, stews are best frozen in foil containers which can be used in the oven, or in foil-lined containers, so that the foil may be formed into a parcel and removed from the original container for easy storage. For reheating, the foil is removed, the stew returned to its original oven-container and heated. If cartons are preferred, the stew may be transferred to an oven dish, or reheated in a double boiler or over direct heat if curdling is not likely to occur.

It is best to freeze cooked meat dishes for no longer than 1 month. Many do have a longer life, but it is intelligent to turn over this type of dish fairly frequently and keep plenty of variety in the freezer. Perhaps the greatest advantage of making these dishes is that double quantities can be prepared with one portion eaten immediately and the remainder frozen for future use, thus saving both preparation time and fuel.

MEAT PIES

For fuller details of freezing pies, refer to Chapter 16 "Pies and Pie Fillings". It is possible to freeze meat pies completely cooked so that they need only be heated. Preparation time is however saved if the meat filling is cooked and cooled, then topped with pastry to be frozen in its raw state. The time taken to cook the pastry is enough to heat the meat filling, and is little longer than the time needed to reheat the whole pie.

Pies are most easily frozen in foil containers which can be used in the oven for final cooking. If a bottom crust is used, sogginess will be prevented if the bottom pastry is brushed with melted lard or butter just before filling.

Individual pies may be prepared, and also such items as sausages rolls and Cornish pasties. Pies should be reheated at 400°F. for required time according to size. Storage time: 1–2 months.

MEAT BALLS

These are particularly useful for freezer storage, since they can be used in sauce and with spaghetti or rice for quick meals. They may be frozen in bags, or in containers with the layers divided by Cellophane or greaseproof paper for easy handling. Meat balls need not be thawed, but fried quickly in hot fat, or heated in tomato or brown sauce.

MEAT LOAF

2 EGGS	1½ TEASPOONS SALT
½ PINT MILK	½ TEASPOON PEPPER
6 OUNCES SOFT WHITE	2 POUNDS MINCED CHUCK
BREADCRUMBS	STEAK

Beat eggs lightly with a fork, then work in milk, breadcrumbs, seasonings and mince. Mix well and put into a pan lined with foil. Use a pan 9 inches × 9 inches × 2 inches and let the foil extend 6 inches above the top of the pan. Pack the meat down well, fold over foil and form parcel and put into freezer. When meat is frozen, remove parcel from pan for storage. To bake, remove foil from meat, put meat into pan and bake at 350°F. (Gas Mark 4) for 1 hour 40 minutes. Serve in squares with tomato sauce or gravy. The meat loaf may also be baked before freezing at the same temperature; reheating will take 30 minutes at 400°F. (Gas Mark 6), or the loaf may be thawed and eaten cold or used in sandwiches. Storage time: 1 month.

STUFFED PEPPERS

Fill uncooked blanched peppers (see Chapter 13 "Vegetables and Herbs") with meat loaf mixture. Put into foil containers, cover and freeze. Bake in covered container at 350°F. (Gas Mark 4) for 1 hour 20 minutes. Storage time: 1 month.

STUFFED CABBAGE

I POUND MINCED CHUCK STEAK	I TEASPOON CHOPPED PARSLEY
I OUNCE BUTTER	SALT AND PEPPER
I SMALL ONION	STOCK
2 TABLESPOONS COOKED RICE	12 MEDIUM-SIZED CABBAGE LEAVES

Cook meat and onion gently in butter until meat browns. Mix with rice, parsley and seasonings and enough stock to moisten and cook for 5 minutes. Blanch cabbage leaves in boiling water for 2 minutes and drain well. Put a spoonful of filling on each leaf, and form into a parcel, put parcels close together in a covered oven dish and cover with stock. Cook at 350°F. (Gas Mark 4) for 45 minutes. Cool, pack into containers and freeze. Reheat in a double boiler or in moderate oven. The dish is improved if the stock is well seasoned and thickened with cornflour. Storage time: 1 month.

MEAT BALLS (WITH SPAGHETTI OR RICE)

$\frac{3}{4}$ POUND MINCED BEEF	I SMALL CHOPPED ONION
$\frac{1}{4}$ POUND MINCED PORK	$1\frac{1}{2}$ TEASPOONS SALT
2 OUNCES DRY WHITE BREADCRUMBS	$\frac{1}{4}$ TEASPOON PEPPER
$\frac{1}{2}$ PINT CREAMY MILK	BUTTER

Mix together beef and pork, and soak breadcrumbs in milk. Cook onion in a little butter until golden. Mix together meat, crumbs and onion with seasonings until well blended. Shape into 1 inch balls, using 2 tablespoons dipped in cold water. Fry balls in butter until evenly brown, shaking pan to make balls round. Drain and cool, and pack in bags or in boxes with greaseproof paper between layers. In Sweden these are eaten cold, and may be used in this way after thawing. The meatballs may be quickly fried in hot fat to serve, or they may be heated in tomato sauce or gravy to serve with spaghetti or rice. Storage time: 1 month.

To freeze spaghetti or rice, slightly undercook in boiling salted water. Drain well, and cool under cold running water in a sieve. Shake as dry as possible, pack into bags and freeze. To serve, put into pan of boiling water, and bring water back to boil, then reduce heat until spaghetti or rice is just tender, the time depending on the state in which it has been frozen. Rice may also be reheated in a frying pan with a little melted butter.

CURRY

The best method for freezing is to incorporate cooked meat in a curry sauce (see Chapter 10 "Poultry" recipe for Chicken in Curry Sauce). When the sauce has been made, the pan should be removed from the heat and the cut-up cold meat left to soak in the sauce; when cool, pack into cartons and freeze. Reheat over low heat or in a double boiler. Storage time: 1 month.

BEEF GALANTINE

1 POUND CHUCK STEAK	1 TEASPOON CHOPPED
4 OUNCES BACON	PARSLEY
4 OUNCES FINE WHITE	1 TEASPOON CHOPPED THYME
BREADCRUMBS	SALT AND PEPPER
	2 EGGS

Mince steak and bacon and mix with other ingredients, moistening with egg. Put into a loaf tin and steam for 3 hours. Cool under weights, turn out, wrap in moisture-vapour-proof wrapping and freeze. This is best thawed in a refrigerator overnight, and may be coated with brown breadcrumbs before serving. Storage time: 1 month.

STEAK AND KIDNEY PIE

1 POUND STEAK	¾ PINT STOCK
4 OUNCES KIDNEY	8 OUNCES FLAKY OR SHORT
1 TABLESPOON CORNFLOUR	PASTRY
SALT AND PEPPER	

Cut steak and kidney into neat pieces, and fry until brown in a little melted dripping. Add seasoning and stock and simmer for 2 hours. Thicken gravy with corn-flour and pour mixture into foil dish. When meat is cool, cover with pastry, pack and freeze. Bake at 400°F. (Gas Mark 6) until pastry is cooked and golden. Storage time: 1 month.

BEEF IN WINE

3 POUNDS SHIN BEEF	SPRIG OF THYME
1½ OUNCES BUTTER	SPRIG OF PARSLEY
1½ OUNCES OIL	1 TABLESPOON TOMATO
1 MEDIUM ONION	PUREE
2 GARLIC CLOVES	STOCK
2 OUNCES BACON	½ PINT RED WINE

Cut meat into slices and cover very lightly with seasoned flour. Fry in a mixture of butter and oil until meat is just coloured, then add sliced onion, crushed garlic and bacon in small strips. Add herbs and wine and cook quickly until liquid is reduced to half. Work in tomato puree and just cover in stock, cover and simmer for 2 hours. Remove herbs and cool. Pack into containers and freeze. Reheat in double boiler. Storage time: 1 month.

JELLIED BEEF

4 POUNDS BEEF BRISKET	½ PINT STOCK
8 OUNCES LEAN BACON	PINCH OF NUTMEG
SALT AND PEPPER	PARSLEY, THYME, BAYLEAF
1 PINT RED WINE	4 ONIONS
2 OUNCES BUTTER	4 CARROTS
2 OUNCES OIL	1 CALF'S FOOT

See there is not too much fat on the beef, and that it is firmly tied. Leave to soak in wine for 2 hours after seasoning all over with salt and pepper. Drain meat and brown in mixture of butter and oil, then put into a casserole with wine, stock, nutmeg, herbs, onions, carrots and split calf's foot. Cover and cook at 325°F. (Gas Mark 3) for 3 hours. Cool slightly and slice beef and put into containers with sliced vegetables. Strain liquid and cool, pour over, cover and freeze. Thaw in refrigerator to eat cold, or heat in covered dish in moderate oven (350°F. or Gas Mark 4) for 45 minutes. Storage time: 1 month.

Chapter 10

POULTRY

All poultry freezes well and is a useful freezer standby. While uncooked birds may be frozen whole or in joints, cooked poultry also freezes excellently. This is of course a useful way of making leftover poultry appetising by freezing it immediately in the form of pies, casseroles or patés, and this is also the answer for the older tougher bird.

PREPARATION FOR FREEZING

Birds to be frozen should be in perfect condition, and should be starved for 24 hours before killing, then hung and bled well. When the bird is plucked, it is important to avoid skin damage; if scalding, beware of over-scalding which may increase the chance of freezer-burn (grey spots occurring during storage). The bird should be cooled in a refrigerator or cold larder for 12 hours, drawn and completely cleaned. With geese and ducks, it is particularly important to see the oil glands are removed as these will cause tainting.

PACKING

A whole bird should be carefully trussed to make a neat shape for packing. Birds may be frozen in halves or joints. When packing pieces, it is not always ideal to pack a complete bird in each package; it may be more useful ultimately if all drumsticks are packaged together, all breasts or all wings, according to the way in which the flesh will be cooked. *Giblets* have a storage life of 2 months, so unless a whole bird is to be used within that time, it is not advisable to pack them inside the bird. Giblets should be cleaned, washed, dried and chilled, then wrapped in moisture-vapour-proof paper or bag, excluding air; frozen in batches, they may be used for soup, stews or pies. *Livers* should be treated in the same way and packaged in batches for use in omelettes, risotto or paté.

Bones of poultry joints should be padded with a small piece of paper or foil to avoid tearing freezer wrappings. Joints should be divided by two layers of Cellophane. Bones of young birds may turn brown in storage, but this does not affect flavour or quality.

STORAGE LIFE

Geese and ducks have a storage life of 6–8 months; turkey and chicken frozen whole 8–12 months, and in pieces 6–10 months. Giblets and livers should not be kept longer than 2 months.

STUFFING

Stuffing can be put into a bird before freezing, but it is not advisable as the storage life of stuffing is only about 1 month. Pork sausage stuffing should not be used, and if a bird must be stuffed, a breadcrumb stuffing is best. It is better to package stuffing specially, but this is unneccessary as a stuffing may be prepared during the thawing time of the bird.

COOKED POULTRY

Old birds such as boiling chickens are best cooked, and the meat stripped from the bones; this meat can then be frozen, or made at once into pies or casseroles, while the carcase can be simmered in the cooking liquid to make strong stock for freezing. Slices of cooked poultry can be frozen on their own, or in sauce (the latter method is preferable to prevent drying out). If the meat is frozen without sauce, slices should be divided by two sheets of Cellophane and then closely packed together excluding air. Roast and fried poultry frozen to be eaten cold are not particularly successful; on thawing they tend to exude moisture and become flabby.

THAWING

Uncooked poultry tastes far better if allowed to thaw

completely before cooking. Thawing in the refrigerator will allow slow, even thawing; thawing at room temperature will be twice as fast. A 4–5 pound chicken will thaw overnight in a refrigerator, and will take 4 hours at room temperature. A turkey weighing 9 pounds will take 36 hours; as much as 3 days should be allowed for a very large bird. A thawed bird may be stored up to 24 hours longer in a refrigerator, but no more.

All poultry should be thawed in unopened freezer wrapping. In emergency, poultry may be thawed quickly by leaving the bag immersed in running cold water, allowing 30 minutes per pound thawing time.

POULTRY STUFFING

2 OUNCES SUET	I TEASPOON CHOPPED THYME
4 OUNCES FRESH BREADCRUMBS	GRATED RIND OF ½ LEMON
	SALT AND PEPPER
2 TEASPOONS CHOPPED PARSLEY	I MEDIUM EGG

Grate suet and mix all ingredients together binding with the egg. Pack into cartons or moisture-vapour-proof bags, seal, label and freeze. The storage life of this stuffing is 1 month. For a storage life of 2 weeks, 2 ounces chopped bacon may be added. It is not advisable to stuff poultry before freezing, but if this must be done, the stuffing must be very cold before putting into the bird, and the bird should also be stuffed in a very cold place. The freezer life of a bird thus prepared will be only that of the stuffing (i.e. 1 month). This mixture may be deep-fried, cooled and packed as forcemeat balls; to use, these can be put into a roasting tin with poultry or into a casserole 10 minutes before serving time.

OVEN-FRIED CHICKEN

2 POUNDS CHICKEN PIECES	I TEASPOON SALT
¼ PINT SOUR CREAM	PINCH OF PEPPER
I DESSERT SPOON LEMON JUICE	PINCH OF PAPRIKA
	2 CLOVES GARLIC
I TEASPOON WORCESTER SAUCE	4 OUNCES BREADCRUMBS

If commercial sour cream is not available, sour fresh cream with 1 teaspoon lemon juice to ¼ pint cream. Mix together cream, lemon juice and seasonings, chopping garlic finely. Wipe chicken pieces and cover completely in sour cream mixture. Coat in breadcrumbs and arrange pieces in greased baking dish. Bake at 350°F. (Gas Mark 4) for 45 minutes until chicken is tender and golden. Cool chicken completely, wrap individually or in a single layer, seal, label and freeze. To serve chicken, place wrapped frozen chicken in oven and bake at 450°F. (Gas Mark 8) for 45 minutes (individually wrapped chicken pieces will take 30 minutes). Uncover chicken and bake 10 minutes longer to crisp. This method of preparing gives a tender result. It may not save much preparation time, but does mean the frozen product can be cooking without any trouble while time is given to preparing vegetables or a pudding; this is also a very good picnic dish which is best reheated following instructions in this recipe and wrapped in clean foil for carrying. Storage time: 1 month.

CHICKEN PIE

5 POUND BOILING FOWL	1 POUND CARROTS
2 CELERY STALKS	2 POUNDS SHELLED PEAS
1 MEDIUM ONION	6 OUNCES MUSHROOMS
½ SLICED LEMON	½ PINT THIN CREAM
2 SPRIGS PARSLEY	PINCH OF NUTMEG
1 BAY LEAF	2 OUNCES CORNFLOUR
SALT AND PEPPER	FLAKY PASTRY

Simmer chicken in water for 2½ hours with celery, onion, lemon, parsley, bay leaf, salt and pepper. Let chicken cool in stock, and cut flesh from bones in neat cubes. Slice carrots and cook carrots and peas for 15 minutes. Cook sliced mushrooms in a little butter. Drain vegetables and mix with chicken flesh. Measure out 2 pints chicken stock and make a sauce with cornflour, a seasoning of nutmeg, salt and pepper to taste, and stir in thin cream without boiling. Simmer for 3 minutes until smooth, pour over chicken mixture and cool completely. Divide mixture into foil pie plates and cover with flaky pastry. Wrap, seal, label and freeze. To serve, unwrap pies, make gashes in pastry to release steam, and put dishes on baking sheet. Bake at 450°F. (Gas Mark 8) for 40 minutes. This quantity of filling will make eight 6 inch diameter pies. The filling mixture may also be made up omitting the cream and frozen as a stew to be served with rice or noodles.

CHICKEN IN CURRY SAUCE

3 POUNDS CHICKEN PIECES
2 MEDIUM ONIONS
1 TABLESPOON CURRY
  POWDER
1 TABLESPOON CORNFLOUR

1 PINT CHICKEN STOCK
  (FROM COOKING CHICKEN
  PIECES)
1 TABLESPOON VINEGAR
1 TABLESPOON BROWN SUGAR
1 TABLESPOON CHUTNEY
1 TABLESPOON SULTANAS

Simmer chicken in water until tender, drain off stock and keep chicken warm. Slice onions, and fry in a little butter until soft. Add curry powder and cook for 1 minute. Gradually add chicken stock and cornflour blended with a little cold water. Add remaining ingredients and simmer 5 minutes. Add chicken pieces and simmer 15 minutes. Cool completely, put into containers, seal, label and freeze. To serve, turn out into top of double boiler and heat through. This is not a classic curry recipe, but is a serviceable one for the freezer, and makes a change from the rather bland chicken dishes which are so often frozen.

POTTED CHICKEN

COLD ROAST CHICKEN   SALT AND PEPPER

Strip chicken from bones and simmer bones in a little water to make strong stock. Mince chicken finely and pack into small foil containers. Pour over stock and chill. Put a piece of foil on each container, wrap, seal, label and freeze. To serve, thaw at room temperature for 1 hour and turn out; cut in slices for salad, or serve in sandwiches. Use immediately after thawing.

CHICKEN LIVER PATE

8 OUNCES CHICKEN LIVERS	I SMALL ONION
3 OUNCES FAT BACON	I EGG
2 CRUSHED GARLIC CLOVES	SALT AND PEPPER

Cut livers in small pieces and cut up bacon and onion. Cook bacon and onion in a little butter until onion is just soft, add livers and cook gently for 10 minutes. Put mixture through a very fine mincer and season with salt and pepper, crushed garlic and mix with beaten egg. Put mixture into foil containers, stand them in baking tin of water and cook at 300°F. (Gas Mark 4) for 1 hour. Cool completely, cover each container with a circle of foil, wrap, seal, label and freeze. Thaw at room temperature for 1 hour before serving. Use immediately after thawing. Storage time: 1 month.

CREAMED TURKEY

COOKED TURKEY	WHITE SAUCE

Cut cooked turkey into small neat pieces and bind with white sauce made with half turkey stock and half milk, and thickened with cornflour. Cool completely, pack in containers, seal, label and freeze. Reheat in a double boiler to serve with toast or rice, with the addition of a few mushrooms, peas or peppers. This mixture can also be used as a filling for pies or flans.

TURKEY ROLL

12 OUNCES COLD TURKEY	SALT AND PEPPER
8 OUNCES COOKED HAM	½ TEASPOON MIXED HERBS
I SMALL ONION	I LARGE EGG
PINCH OF MACE	BREADCRUMBS

Mince turkey, ham and onion finely and mix with mace, salt and pepper and herbs. Bind with beaten egg. Put into greased dish or tin, cover and steam for 1 hour. While still warm, roll in breadcrumbs. Cool completely, wrap, seal, label and freeze. To serve, thaw at room temperature for 1 hour, and slice to serve with salads. The "roll" may be cooked in a loaf tin, a large cocoa tin lined with paper, or a stone marmalade jar. Storage time; 1 month.

GAME

Game of all kinds, including venison, hare and rabbit, freezes extremely well. The game dealer freezes birds in feather for sale at a later date, but in the home this means plucking and cleaning after thawing which is difficult and unpleasant, and as with all other frozen items, it is best to prepare the food in the state in which it will be most immediately useful. Game birds and animals may be frozen raw, birds can be roast then frozen to be eaten cold after thawing, or game may be turned into such items as casseroles, pies and patés before freezing.

In the main, it is best to freeze raw those birds or animals which are young and well shot. Roast game is useful to freeze and eat cold, but on thawing exudes moisture so that the flesh is flabby. Old or badly shot game is best converted immediately into made-up dishes for which recipes are given later in this chapter.

All game for freezing should be kept cool after shooting. Game should be hung to its required state before freezing, as hanging after thawing will result in the flesh going bad. *Grouse, pheasant* and *partridge* should be plucked and drawn before freezing. *Plover, quail, snipe* and *woodcock* should be plucked but not drawn, though any waterfowl fed on fish should be drawn. *Hare* and *rabbit* are handled like poultry. *Venison* is treated as beef, and is best if aged for 5 to 6 days before freezing if the carcase is in good condition and chilled quickly after shooting.

GAME BIRDS
All game birds should be kept cool between shooting and freezing; care should be taken to remove as much shot as possible, and to make sure shot wounds are thoroughly

clean. Birds should be bled as soon as shot, kept cool, and hung to individual taste. After plucking and drawing, the cavity should be thoroughly washed and drained and the body wiped with a damp cloth. The birds should then be packed, cooled and frozen, as for poultry (see Chapter 10 "Poultry"). Game will keep in the freezer 6–8 months.

HARES AND RABBITS

Hares and rabbits should be beheaded and bled as soon as possible and hung for 24 hours in a cool place. Skin and clean, washing cavity well, and wipe with a damp cloth. Cut into joints and wrap each piece in Cellophane, excluding air, then pack joints together in moisture-vapour-proof bag or paper, seal, label and freeze (see Chapter 10 "Poultry"). Hares and rabbits will keep in the freezer 6–8 months.

VENISON

Venison needs careful butchering, but if help is not immediately available, the carcase should be kept in good condition, the shot wounds carefully cleaned, and the animal kept as cold as possible. The venison should be beheaded and bled, skinned and cleaned, and the interior washed and wiped. Hanging should take place in a very cool place (preferably just above freezing point) with the belly propped open so air can circulate. 5 to 6 days' hanging will make the meat tender. The meat should be cut in joints, packed like meat (see Chapter 9 "Meat"), sealed, labelled and frozen. Since this is a large animal, it is best to keep only the good joints whole. The rest of the meat can be minced to freeze raw for later use as hamburgers and mince, or can be casseroled or made into pies and frozen in this form. Since the meat is inclined to dryness, it is often marinaded before cooking. The marinade should be poured over the meat while it is thawing. Venison will keep in the freezer 8–10 months.

THAWING GAME

All game should be thawed in the sealed freezer package; thawing in a refrigerator is more uniform, but will take longer. In a refrigerator, allow 5 hours per pound thawing time; at room temperature, allow 2 hours per pound. Start cooking as soon as game is thawed and still cold to prevent loss of juices. The following recipes have proved their freezer value.

VENISON MARINADE

½ PINT RED WINE
½ PINT VINEGAR

I LARGE SLICED ONION
PARSLEY, THYME, BAYLEAF

Mix these ingredients together and cover frozen venison joint as it thaws, turning meat frequently. The marinade may be used for cooking the meat, but if roasting is preferred, the meat is best covered with strips of fat bacon before roasting (the loin and haunch are the best cuts for roasting; shoulder and neck can be casseroled; minced venison is excellent for hamburgers and for cottage pie).

POT ROAST PIGEONS

4 PIGEONS
SEASONED FLOUR
BUTTER

¼ PINT STOCK
I TEASPOON MIXED HERBS

Clean pigeons and wipe with a cloth. Cover lightly in flour and brown birds in a little butter. Add herbs and stock and cover tightly, cooking very gently on top of the stove or in the oven for 1 hour. Cool quickly and pack into container (the birds can be put into a foil dish with juices round them, then into moisture-vapour-proof bag), seal, label and freeze. To serve, put into a casserole or tightly covered saucepan and heat in moderate oven or on moderate burner (about 50 minutes in oven). This is a good method for birds of uncertain age. Serve them with pan juices, bread sauce and game chips.

PIGEON PIE

| 6 PIGEONS | SALT, PEPPER AND MACE |
| 8 OUNCES CHUCK STEAK | 8 OUNCES PASTRY |

This may be prepared by two methods; the filling and pastry can be cooked before freezing, or the filling cooked and covered with uncooked pastry. It is *not* possible to freeze both contents and pastry uncooked satisfactorily as the thawing and cooking times do not give enough time for both to cook well. Small mushrooms and/or hard-cooked egg yolks make pleasant additions to the pie. Remove the breasts from the pigeons with a sharp knife and put into a saucepan with the steak cut into small pieces. Season with salt, pepper and mace and just cover with water. Simmer with lid on for 1 hour. Cool completely. Put into foil baking dishes and cover with pastry sealing well. *Either* wrap, seal, label and freeze at once *or* bake at 425°F. (Gas Mark 7) for 30 minutes, cool completely, wrap, seal, label and freeze. To serve *if pastry is uncooked,* bake unthawed pie at 400°F. (Gas Mark 6) for 45 minutes. *If pastry is cooked,* bake unthawed pie at 350°F. (Gas Mark 4) for 30 minutes.

HOT WATER CRUST GAME PIES

These are normally eaten cold and can be frozen baked or unbaked, but there are obvious risks attached to freezing them. The pastry is made with hot water, and the pie may be completely baked, and cooled before freezing; however the jelly must be added just before the pie is to be served. The easiest way to do this is to freeze the stock separately at the time of making the pie, and when the pie is thawing (taking about 4 hours) the partially thawed pie can be filled with boiling stock through the hole in the crust, and this will speed up the thawing process. The second method involves freezing the pie unbaked, partially thawing then baking. However this means the uncooked meat will be in contact with the warm uncooked pastry during the making process, and unless the pie is very carefully handled while cooling, there is severe risk of dangerous organisms entering the meat. On balance it would seem preferable not to freeze this type of pie but to make it as required, if necessary from frozen game.

HARE PATÉ

1½ POUNDS UNCOOKED HARE	¾ POUND MINCED PORK AND
½ POUND FAT BACON	VEAL
3 TABLESPOONS BRANDY	SALT, PEPPER, NUTMEG
	1 EGG

This recipe may also be used for rabbit or for a mixture of game. Mix pieces of hare and bacon and put into a dish sprinkled with brandy. Leave for an hour, then mince with pork and veal. Season well with salt, pepper and nutmeg, add egg and mix well. Press mixture into a buttered container, cover with greased paper and lid, and stand dish in a tin of water. Bake at 400°F. (Gas Mark 6) allowing 40 minutes per pound of mixture. When the paté is done, a skewer will come out clean and the juices will not run. Leave under weights until paté is cold. Pack mixture into small jars or foil containers, cover with foil, put into moisture-vapour-proof bag, seal, label and freeze. If a large amount of paté is to be eaten at once, it may be left in a large container for freezing. Once thawed, it has a short life, and it is thus usually easier to freeze in small containers which will thaw in about 1 hour at room temperature and will be eaten quickly. If the paté is cooked in small containers however, it may be rather dry.

PHEASANT PATE

8 OUNCES CALVES LIVER	1 COOKED PHEASANT
4 OUNCES BACON	POWDERED CLOVES AND
1 SMALL ONION	ALLSPICE
SALT AND PEPPER	

Lightly fry liver and bacon and put through mincer with onion. Season well with salt and pepper. Take meat from pheasant in neat pieces and season well with powdered cloves and allspice. Put a layer of liver mixture into dish, then a layer of pheasant, and continue in layers finishing with the liver mixture. Cover and steam for 2 hours, then cool with heavy weights on top. When cold, wrap in moisture-vapour-proof wrapping, seal, label and freeze.

POTTED GROUSE

2 OLD GROUSE	BUTTER
1 CARROT	BUNCH OF MIXED HERBS
1 ONION	SALT AND PEPPER
2 OUNCES STREAKY BACON	

Slice carrots and onions and cut bacon in neat pieces, and fry in butter until golden. Put into the bottom of a casserole with herbs, plenty of salt and pepper and the grouse. Cover with stock and cook at 300°F. (Gas Mark 2) for 2½ hours. Remove carrot. Put meat from grouse with onion, bacon and a little stock through a mincer, then pound or liquidise to a smooth paste. Press into small containers, cover with foil, put in moisture-vapour-proof wrapping, seal, label and freeze. A small glass of port improves this paste. Thaw for 1 hour at room temperature and serve with hot toast.

GROUSE CASSEROLE

2 GROUSE	PARSLEY, THYME AND
8 OUNCES LEAN BACON	BAYLEAF
1 SMALL ONION	½ PINT STOCK
1 CARROT	1 WINEGLASS RED WINE
1 STICK CELERY	SALT AND PEPPER

Flour the grouse very lightly and cook in a little butter until both sides are golden. Slice the bacon and vegetables. Take out grouse and put into casserole. Cook bacon and vegetables in butter until just soft and add to casserole. Make sauce using the pan drippings and stock, thickening with a little cornflour (about 1 dessertspoon). Season to taste with salt and pepper and pour over grouse. Cover and cook in low oven (325°F. or Gas Mark 3) for 2 hours. Add wine and continue cooking for 30 minutes. Cool completely, put into container, seal, label and freeze. To serve, transfer to casserole and heat at 350°F. (Gas Mark 4) for 45 minutes; split grouse in half and serve with vegetables and gravy and a garnish of watercress.

PHEASANT IN CIDER

1 OLD PHEASANT	½ PINT CIDER
1 POUND COOKING APPLES	1 CLOVE GARLIC
8 OUNCES ONIONS	BUNCH OF MIXED HERBS
2 OUNCES BUTTER	SALT AND PEPPER

Cut the apples in quarters after peeling and coring and put into a casserole. Slice onions and cook in butter until soft and transparent. Put pheasant on to apples and cover with onions. Pour on cider and put in herbs and crushed garlic clove, and season with salt and pepper. Cover and cook at 325°F. (Gas Mark 3) for 2 hours. Cool and remove herbs. Put pheasant into freezer container and put casserole liquid through a sieve. Pour over pheasant, cover, seal, label and freeze. To serve, put into casserole and cook at 350°F. for 1 hour.

PIGEON CASSEROLE

2 PIGEONS	SALT AND PEPPER
8 OUNCES CHUCK STEAK	1 TABLESPOON REDCURRANT
2 RASHERS BACON	JELLY
BUTTER	1 TABLESPOON LEMON JUICE
½ PINT STOCK	1 TABLESPOON CORNFLOUR
2 OUNCES BUTTON MUSHROOMS	

Cut pigeons in halves and the steak in cubes, and cut bacon in small pieces. Melt butter and cook pigeons, steak and bacon until just coloured. Put into a casserole with stock, sliced mushrooms, salt and pepper. Cover and cook at 325°F. (Gas Mark 3) for 2 hours. Stir in redcurrant jelly, lemon juice and cornflour blended with a little water, and continue cooking for 30 minutes. Cool and transfer to freezer container. When cold, cover, seal, label and freeze. To serve, transfer to casserole and cook at 350°F. (Gas Mark 4) for 45 minutes.

JUGGED HARE

1 HARE	SALT AND PEPPER
1 CARROT	4 PINTS WATER
1 ONION	2 OUNCES BUTTER
1 BLADE MACE	2 TABLESPOONS OLIVE OIL
PARSLEY, THYME, BAYLEAF	1 TABLESPOON CORNFLOUR
4 CLOVES	½ PINT PORT

Soak head, heart and liver of hare for 1 hour in cold salted water. Put into a pan with carrot, onion, mace, herbs, cloves, salt and pepper and water, and bring to boil. Skim, then simmer for 3 hours, skimming often. Lightly coat pieces of hare in seasoned flour and brown in a mixture of hot butter and oil. Put into a casserole. Mix cornflour with a little water and add to strained stock. Simmer until this has reduced to 3 pints, then add to casserole. Cover and cook at 345°F. (Gas Mark 3) for 4 hours until hare is tender. Remove hare pieces and cool. Add port to gravy and simmer until gravy is of coating consistency, then cool. Put portions into containers, cover with gravy leaving ¾ inch headspace, cover, seal, label and freeze. To thaw, put into casserole and heat at 350°F. (Gas Mark 4) for 45 minutes, adding frozen forcemeat balls 10 minutes before serving time (see Chapter 10 "Poultry": recipe for poultry stuffing).

Chapter 12

FISH AND SHELLFISH

Only really fresh fish can be frozen, since it should be processed within 24 hours, and therefore it is not advisable to freeze shop-purchased fish. It is possible to freeze smoked fish such as bloaters, kippers and haddock, and these can be useful to vary meals, and good quality smoked fish can often be purchased from the curers by post.

Cooked fish can be frozen in sauces or pies, or ready-fried, but is not worth the trouble. Fish should never be overcooked and the time taken to reheat will not only spoil flavour and rob the fish of any nutritive value, but will also take as long as the original cooking.

Fatty fish (i.e. haddock, halibut, herring, mackerel, salmon, trout, turbot) will keep a maximum of 4 months. White fish (i.e. cod, plaice, sole, whiting) will keep a maximum of 6 months. Shell fish are best stored no longer than 1 month. It is really better to keep fish only a minimum of time in the freezer.

CLEANING THE FISH
Since the fish must be fresh, it will be necessary to clean home-caught fish ready for freezing. The fish should be killed at once, scaled if necessary and fins removed. Small fish can be left whole; large fish should have heads and tails removed, or may be divided into steaks. Flat fish and herrings are best gutted, and flat fish may be skinned and filleted. The fish should be washed well in salted water during cleaning to remove blood and membrances, but fatty fish should be washed in fresh water.

FREEZING METHODS
There are four ways of preparing fish for freezing, the first two being the most common.

1. *Dry Pack.*

Separate pieces of fish with double thickness of Cellophane, wrap in moisture-vapour-proof paper, carton or bag, seal and freeze. Be sure the paper is in close contact with the fish to exclude air which will dry the fish and make it tasteless. Freeze quickly on the floor of the freezer.

2. *Brine Pack.*

This is not suitable for fatty fish, as salt tends to oxidise and lead to rancidity. Dip fish into cold salted water (1 tablespoon salt to 1 quart water), drain, wrap and seal. Do not keep brine-dipped fish longer than 3 months.

3. *Acid Pack.*

Citric acid preserves the colour and flavour of fish; ascorbic acid is an anti-oxidant which stops the development of rancidity in fish which can cause off-flavours and smells. A chemist can provide an ascorbic-citric acid powder, to be diluted in a proportion of 1 part powder to 100 parts of water. Dip fish into this solution, drain, wrap and seal.

4. *Solid Ice Pack.*

Several small fish, steaks or fillets can be covered with water in refrigerator trays or loaf tins and frozen into solid blocks. Fish should be separated by double paper as usual, and the ice blocks removed from pan, wrapped in freezer paper and stored. The fish may also be frozen in a solid ice pack in large waxed tubs; cover the fish completely to within ½ inch of container top and crumple a piece of Cellophane over the top of the fish before closing the lid. There is no particular advantage to this solid ice method except in a saving of containers and wrapping material.

LARGE WHOLE FISH

Sometimes a large whole fish may be wanted, and it can be frozen whole, but is best protected by "glazing". Salmon and salmon trout are obvious examples, or perhaps a haddock or halibut to serve stuffed for a large party. To glaze a large fish, it should first be cleaned, then place the *unwrapped* fish against the freezer wall in the coldest possible part of the freezer. When the fish is frozen solid, dip very quickly into very cold water so a thin coating of ice will form. Return fish to freezer for an hour, and repeat process. Continue until ice has built up to $\frac{1}{4}$ inch thickness. The fish can be stored without wrappings for 2 weeks, but is better wrapped in freezer paper for longer storage.

SMOKED FISH
Bloaters, kippers, and haddock can be wrapped and frozen and will keep for 1 year. No special preparation is necessary.

SHELLFISH
Freshly caught shellfish may be frozen immediately after cooking. Scallops and oysters are frozen raw. Shrimps may be frozen when cooked, or potted in butter.

Crab.
Cook crab, drain and cool thoroughly. Clean, and remove all edible meat. Pack into bags or cartons, leaving $\frac{1}{2}$ inch headspace. Seal and freeze. Thaw in container and serve very cold.

Lobster and Crayfish.
Cook fish, cool and split. Remove meat from shell, pack into bags or cartons, leaving $\frac{1}{2}$ inch headspace. Seal and freeze. Thaw in container and serve cold.

Oysters and Scallops.
Wash in salt water and open carefully (in the case of oysters retaining the juice in a separate container). Wash fish in salt water, allowing a proportion of 1 teaspoon salt to 1 pint water. Pack into cartons, covering oysters with their own juice and scallops with water. See fish are completely covered by liquid, and allow $\frac{1}{2}$ inch headspace in cartons. Seal and freeze. Oysters may be eaten raw or cooked; scallops cooked.

Shrimps and Prawns.

Cook and cool in cooking water. Remove shells, pack tightly in bags or cartons, leaving $\frac{1}{2}$ inch headspace, seal and freeze. Both shrimps and prawns may be frozen in their shells with heads removed, but there is no advantage to this method as they must later be prepared for use before serving.

THAWING AND COOKING

All fish should be thawed slowly in unopened wrappings. 1 pound or 1 pint package takes about 3 hours in room temperature or 6 hours in a refrigerator. Except for frying, complete thawing is not necessary. Frozen fish may be used for boiling, steaming, grilling or frying.

Commercially prepared cooked fish products such as fishcakes and potted shrimps are excellent taken direct from the shop freezer to the home freezer. Some people may prefer to prepare their own.

FISH CAKES

8 OUNCES COOKED WHITE FISH	1 OUNCE BUTTER
8 OUNCES MASHED POTATO	SALT AND PEPPER
2 TEASPOONS CHOPPED PARSLEY	EGG

Mix flaked fish, potato, parsley, melted butter, salt and pepper together, and bind with egg. Divide the mixture into eight portions and form into flat rounds. Coat with egg and breadcrumbs and fry until golden. Cool quickly, pack and freeze. To serve, thaw by reheating in oven or frying pan.

POTTED SHRIMPS

SHRIMPS	SALT AND PEPPER
BUTTER	GROUND MACE AND CLOVES

Cook freshly caught shrimps, cool in cooking liquid, and shell. Pack tightly into waxed cartons. Melt butter, season with salt, pepper, and a little mace and cloves.

Cool butter and pour over shrimps. Chill until cold, cover, seal and freeze. Some people like to use a little cayenne pepper to season.

Chapter 13

VEGETABLES AND HERBS

Nearly all vegetables freeze extremely well, and this is valuable to the home gardener with excess supplies. Shop-bought vegetables will rarely be at peak condition, but it can be useful to freeze some of the more exotic seasonal delicacies which are imported such as aubergines and peppers. For the large family, preparation time can be saved by freezing such basics as potatoes in the form of chips.

Vegetables which do not freeze well are those which do not retain their crispness i.e. salad greens and radishes. Cucumbers are worth experimenting with in a special pack for salads and sandwiches. Tomatoes, celery and onions can be frozen but are not satisfactory to eat raw and so are best prepared and frozen in a form in which they can aid the cook in saving time when making cooked dishes.

All vegetables to be frozen should be young and tender, and at the peak of perfection. They should be frozen in small quantities, and are therefore best picked and prepared in small amounts. They are best picked in the early morning.

Preparation for freezing vegetables is a little more elaborate than for other raw items for the freezer. The vegetables must be blanched before processing. This is a form of cooking at high heat which stops the working of enzymes (chemical agents in plants) which affect quality, flavour and colour, and nutritive value during storage.

PREPARATION FOR FREEZING

All vegetables should be young and fresh. The faster they are frozen, the better will be the results. All vegetables must first be washed thoroughly in cold water, then cut or sorted into similar sizes. Only 3 pounds of food per cubic foot. of freezer space should be frozen every 6 hours, so only prepare small quantities. If more are picked than can be dealt with, they should be put into polythene bags in a refrigerator.

BLANCHING

There are two forms of blanching, (a) by water; (b) by steam. Steam blanching is not recommended for leafy green vegetables which tend to mat together, and takes longer than water blanching, though it conserves more minerals and vitamins. Blanching should be timed carefully, though inaccuracy will not be disastrous. Too little blanching may result in colour change and in a loss of nutritive value; too much blanching will mean a loss of crispness and fresh flavour.

Water blanching.

Blanch only 1 pound vegetables at a time to ensure thoroughness and to prevent a quick change in the temperature of the water. Use a saucepan holding at least 8 pints of water (see Chapter 6 "Basic Equipment and Packaging Materials"). Bring the water to the boil while the vegetables are being prepared. Put vegetables into a wire basket or a muslin bag and completely immerse in the saucepan of fast boiling water, covering tightly and keeping the heat high under the saucepan. Time blanching from when water returns to boiling point, and check carefully the time needed for each vegetable. As soon as the time has elapsed, remove vegetables and drain at once. Bring water to boiling point again before dealing with another batch of vegetables.

Steam blanching.

Put enough water into saucepan below steamer to prevent boiling dry. Prepare vegetables and when water is fast boiling put wire basket or muslin bag into steamer. Cover tightly, and count steaming time from when the steam escapes from the lid. Steam blanching takes half as long again as water blanching (e.g. 2 minutes water blanching equals 3 minutes steam blanching).

COOLING

Cooling must be done immediately after blanching, and it must be very thorough indeed; before being packed for the freezer the vegetables should be cool right through to the centre. The time taken is generally equal to the blanching time if a large quantity of cold water is used. It is best to ice-chill this water, and it is a good idea to prepare large quantities of ice the day before a vegetable freezing session is planned. Vegetables which are not cooled quickly become mushy as they will go on cooking in their own heat. After cooling, the vegetables should be thoroughly drained, and preferably finished off on absorbent paper.

PACKING

Pack in usable quantities to suit family or entertaining needs. Vegetables may be packed in bags or boxes; the chosen method depends on storage space available as bagged vegetables are more difficult to keep though obviously cheaper to prepare.

Vegetables are normally packed dry, though wet-packing in brine is believed to prevent some vegetables toughening in storage, and non-leafy varieties may be packed in this way. The vegetables are packed into rigid containers to within 1 inch of the top, and then just covered with brine, made in the proportion of 2 table-spoons salt per quart of water, leaving $\frac{1}{2}$ inch headspace. It may be found in hard water areas that home-frozen vegetables are consistently tough, and it is then worth experimenting with this brine method.

THAWING

Best results are obtained from cooking vegetables immediately on removal from the freezer. When cooking unthawed vegetables, break the block into 4 or 5 pieces when removing from the carton to allow heat to penetrate evenly and rapidly.

One or two vegetables such as broccoli and spinach are better for partial thawing, and corn on the cob needs

71

complete thawing (see directions for individual vegetables). Thawed mushrooms become pulpy. If vegetables are thawed, they should be cooked at once. Allow 6 hours in a refrigerator for 1 pound packets, and 3 hours at room temperature for complete thawing.

COOKING

Partial cooking during blanching and the tenderising process produced by temperature changes during storage reduce the final cooking time of frozen vegetables. In general they should cook in one-third to one-half the time allowed for fresh vegetables. Very little water should be used for cooking frozen vegetables, about $\frac{1}{4}$ pint to 1 pound vegetables depending on variety. The water should be boiling, the vegetables covered at once with a lid, and once boiling point is again reached the vegetables simmered for the required time. To avoid loss of flavour in cooking water, vegetables may be steamed, cooked in a double boiler, or baked, or fried.

For baking, the vegetables should be separated and drained, then put into a greased casserole with a knob of butter and seasoning, covered tightly and baked at 350°F. (Gas Mark 4) for 30 minutes. For frying, the vegetables remain frozen, and are put into a heavy frying pan containing 1 ounce melted butter. The pan must be tightly covered and the vegetables cooked gently until they separate, then cooked over moderate heat until cooked through and tender.

Blanching times for individual vegetables are for water blanching.

ARTICHOKES (GLOBE)

Remove outer leaves and wash artichokes very thoroughly. Trim stalks and remove "chokes". Blanch 6 at a time in 4 quarts boiling water with 1 tablespoon lemon juice for 7 minutes. Cool in ice water and drain upside-down on absorbent paper. Pack in boxes, as polythene will be torn. To cook, plunge into boiling water and boil 5 minutes until leaves are tender and easily removed. This is unorthodox, but very satisfactory for artichoke addicts. Those who prefer to freeze only artichoke bottoms for special dishes should remove all green leaves and centre flower, then proceed by the same method, allowing 5 minutes for blanching. Storage time: 1 year.

ASPARAGUS

Remove woody portions and small scales and wash thoroughly. Sort into small, medium and large heads and blanch each separately. Cut asparagus into 6 inch lengths and allow 2 minutes for small spears, 3 minutes for medium spears and 4 minutes for large spears. Cool at once and drain thoroughly. Package in sizes or in mixed bundles according to end-use. Package in boxes lined with moisture-vapour-proof paper. Alternatively, make up bundles alternating heads of asparagus and put into a sheet of freezer paper, folding and sealing. To serve, cook 5 minutes in boiling water. Storage time: 9–12 months.

AUBERGINES (EGG PLANTS)

These are best peeled and cut into 1 inch slices. Blanch 4 minutes, chill and dry in absorbent paper. Pack in cartons, preferably in layers separated by Cellophane. Cook 5 minutes in boiling water. Storage time: 1 year. For short-term storage, aubergines may be frozen ready cooked. They should be fried in deep fat after coating with thin batter or egg and breadcrumbs, well-drained and cooled, and packed in cartons in layers separated by Cellophane. To serve, heat in a slow oven, or part-thaw and deep fry.

For both methods, the aubergines should be mature and medium-sized, with tender seeds, or the results may be rubbery in texture.

BEANS (BROAD)

Use small young beans with tender outer skins. Remove

beans from shell, blanch 1½ minutes, cool and pack in cartons or polythene bags. To serve, cook in boiling salted water for 8 minutes. Storage time: 1 year.

BEANS (FRENCH)
Use tender young beans without strings and cut off tops and tails. Leave small beans whole, or cut into 1 inch pieces. Blanch whole beans 3 minutes, cut beans 2 minutes. Cool and pack in polythene bags. Cook whole beans for 7 minutes in boiling salted water, cut beans for 5 minutes. Storage time: 1 year.

BEANS (RUNNER)
Use tender young beans, and cut into pieces, but do *not* shred finely or the cooked result will be pulpy and tasteless. Blanch 2 minutes, cool and pack in polythene bags. To serve, cook 7 minutes in boiling salted water. Storage time: 1 year.

BEETROOT
Only use very young beetroot, not more than 3 inches in diameter. They must be precooked as short blanching and long storage makes them tough and rubbery. Cook beetroot in boiling water until tender; size will affect cooking time, so put largest ones in water first and add the others in graduated sizes at ten-minute intervals (cooking time will run from 20–50 minutes). Cool quickly in running water, rub off skins and pack. Beetroot under 1 inch in diameter may be frozen whole, larger ones should be sliced or diced. Pack in cartons. Storage time: 6–8 months.

BROCCOLI
Use compact heads with tender stalks not more than 1 inch thick and see heads are uniformly green. Discard any woody stems and trim any outer leaves. Wash very thoroughly, and soak stems in a salt solution (2 teaspoons salt to 8 pints water) to get rid of insects. After 30 minutes, wash stems in clean water. Cut broccoli

into sprigs and blanch 3 minutes for thin stems, 4 minutes for medium stems and 5 minutes for thick stems. Pack into bags or boxes (if using boxes, alternate heads). To serve, cook 8 minutes in boiling water. Storage time: 1 year.

BRUSSELS SPROUTS
Use small compact heads only and grade for size before blanching. Remove discoloured leaves and wash well. Blanch 3 minutes for small sprouts, 4 minutes for medium sprouts, cool and pack in cartons or bags. To serve, cook for 8 minutes in boiling water. Storage time: 1 year.

CABBAGE
Use young crisp cabbage (red cabbage can also be frozen well). Wash very well and shred. Blanch for 1½ minutes and pack in polythene bags. To serve, cook for 8 minutes in boiling water. Frozen cabbage should not be used raw for salads. Storage time: 6 months.

CARROTS
Only freeze very young carrots. Wash them thoroughly and scrape. Carrots may be packed whole, or sliced or diced, but cut-up ones will need ½ inch headspace. Blanch whole small carrots or sliced or diced carrots for 3 minutes. Pack in polythene bags. To serve, cook for 8 minutes in boiling water. Storage time: 1 year.

CAULIFLOWER
Use firm compact heads with close white flowers. Wash thoroughly and break into sprigs not more than 1 inch across. Add the juice of 1 lemon to the blanching water to keep the cauliflower white. Blanch for 3 minutes, cool and pack in lined boxes. To serve, cook for 10 minutes in boiling water. Storage time: 6 months.

CELERY
Celery is not generally recommended for freezing as it cannot then be used raw, but it is useful to freeze for

future stews and soups, or as a vegetable. Use crisp tender stalks and remove any strings. Scrub stalks well and remove all grit and dirt under running water. Cut in 1 inch lengths and blanch for 3 minutes. Pack dry in polythene bags or boxes, or use rigid containers and cover with the flavoured water in which celery has been blanched, leaving $\frac{1}{2}$ inch headspace; this method means the liquid can be used in soups or stews with the celery.

CORN ON THE COB
Correct cooking after freezing is particularly important with corn. The corn must be fresh and tender, and may be frozen as cobs or kernels. Remove leaves and silk threads and grade for size, cutting stems short. Cobs for freezing whole should not be starchy and over-ripe, nor have shrunken or under-sized kernels (these cobs may be used for preparing whole kernels for freezing). Blanch small cobs for 4 minutes, medium cobs for 6 minutes and large cobs for 8 minutes. Cool and dry well on absorbent paper. Pack individual ears in freezer paper and freeze immediately in the coldest part of the freezer (individual ears may then be stored for easy handling in quantities in bags). Whole kernels can be scraped from cobs and packaged in containers leaving $\frac{1}{2}$ inch headspace. Storage time: 1 year.

There are three ways of cooking frozen corn on the cob. *Method a.* Put frozen unwrapped corn in cold water to cover completely and put over high heat. Bring to fastboil, then simmer for 5 minutes. *Method b.* Thaw corn completely in packaging, preferably in refrigerator. Plunge in boiling water and cook 10 minutes. *Method c.* Preheat oven to 350°F. (Gas Mark 4) and roast corn for 20 minutes; or wrap in foil and roast on a barbecue, turning frequently.

CUCUMBER
It is generally considered impossible to freeze cucumber, but this method is successful for those who enjoy cucumber dressed with vinegar. Mix equal quantities of water

and white vinegar and season with $\frac{1}{2}$ teaspoon sugar and $\frac{1}{4}$ teaspoon black pepper to each pint of liquid. Fill plastic boxes with this liquid and thinly slice cucumbers into boxes, filling containers to leave 1 inch headspace. To thaw, put in covered box in refrigerator, and serve well-drained, mixed with thin onion slices and seasoned with salt. Storage time: 2 months.

HERBS
Frozen herbs are not suitable for garnishing, as they become limp on thawing. Their flavour however is useful for sauces, soups and sandwich fillings. The best method is to wash herbs thoroughly and trim from stems, then cut finely and put into ice-cube trays, filling with water. Freeze, then wrap each cube in foil and package quantities in polythene bags. Colour remains good, though flavour is not strong. *Parsley, mint* and *chives* are successfully frozen, and are mainly used for giving colour to finished dishes.

KALE
Young, tender, tightly curled kale may be frozen. Discard any leaves which are discoloured, dry or tough, and wash kale thoroughly. Pull leaves from stems, but do not chop. Blanch for 1 minute, cool and drain (leaves may be chopped after blanching). Pack tightly into bags or into containers leaving $\frac{1}{2}$ inch headspace. To serve, cook in boiling water for 8 minutes. Storage time: 6 months.

KOHLRABI
Use young tender kohlrabi which is not too large and has a mild flavour. Trim, wash and peel, and leave small ones whole or dice larger ones. Blanch whole vegetables for 3 minutes, and diced for 2 minutes. Cool and package in polythene bags or containers, leaving $\frac{1}{2}$ inch headspace for diced vegetables. To serve, cook for 10 minutes in boiling water. Storage time: 1 year.

MARROW
Very young marrow can be frozen unpeeled, cut in $\frac{1}{2}$ inch slices, and blanched for 3 minutes before packing. Older marrows can be peeled and seeded, cooked until soft, and mashed before packing in cartons with $\frac{1}{2}$ inch headspace. The young sliced marrows are best fried in oil with plenty of salt and pepper; the cooked marrow should be reheated in a double boiler with butter and plenty of seasoning, but is a dull vegetable at the best of times and hardly worth freezing.

MUSHROOMS
Very fresh mushrooms may be frozen. Cultivated mushrooms should be wiped clean but not peeled. Mushrooms larger than 1 inch across should be sliced. Stems should be trimmed (long stalks may be frozen separately). Blanch $1\frac{1}{2}$ minutes in water to which 1 tablespoon lemon juice has been added for each 6 pints water. Package cups down in containers, leaving $\frac{1}{2}$ inch headspace. Stalks should be blanched for $1\frac{1}{2}$ minutes. Storage time: 1 year. Mushrooms may also be frozen when ready cooked in butter. Grade into sizes and allow 6 tablespoons butter to each 1 pound mushrooms. Cook 5 minutes, until just cooked. Cool by putting cooking pan into cold water, pack and freeze. Storage time: 3 months.

ONIONS
Onions are hardly worth freezing, though some like the flavour of imported onions and find this worth preserving for out of season use. Onions for serving raw in salads should be served while still frostry; they are best cut in $\frac{1}{4}$ inch slices and packed in freezer paper or foil, with Cellophane dividing the slices, and the packages put into double polythene bags to avoid cross-contamination of flavours. Chopped onions for cooking should be blanched for 2 minutes, chilled, drained and packed in containers, then over-wrapped. Very small whole onions which can later be served in a sauce can either be blanched for 4 minutes before freezing, or cooked until

tender so they need only to be reheated in sauce or stew. Be sure to label the onions with the exact method used as a guide for further cooking operations.

PARSNIPS

Use small young parsnips, trim and peel them, and cut into narrow strips or dice no more than $\frac{1}{2}$ inch thickness. Blanch for 2 minutes and pack in bags or rigid containers. To serve, cook in boiling water for 15 minutes. Storage time: 1 year.

PEAS

Choose young sweet peas, not those which are old and starchy. Shell and blanch for 1 minute, lifting basket in and out of water to distribute heat evenly through layers of peas. Chill immediately and pack in polythene bags or rigid containers. To cook, put in boiling water and cook for 7 minutes. Storage time: 1 year.

PEPPERS

Green and red peppers may be frozen separately or in mixed packages. They may be frozen in halves for stuffing and baking, or sliced for use in stews and sauces. Wash carefully, cut off stems and caps and remove seeds and membranes. Blanch halves for 3 minutes and slices for 2 minutes. Pack in polythene bags or in rigid containers. Thaw before using, allowing $1\frac{1}{2}$ hours at room temperature. Storage time: 1 year. Roast red peppers may also be frozen and are very good. Put peppers under a hot grill until charred, then plunge in cold water and rub off skins. Remove caps and seeds and pack tightly in rigid containers, covering with brine solution (1 tablespoon salt to 1 pint water), leaving 1 inch headspace, and cover. To serve, let the peppers thaw in containers and serve in a little of the brine solution to which has been added 1 tablespoon olive oil, a crushed clove of garlic and a shake of black pepper. They may also be served as an appetiser sliced with anchovies, onion rings and capers and dressed with olive oil and basil.

POTATOES

Potatoes may be frozen in various forms; they are best when small and new, or in the form of croquettes, chips or baked potatoes. New potatoes should be scraped and washed, blanched for 4 minutes, cooled and packed in polythene bags. By this method they can be cooked in 15 minutes and will store for 1 year. Alternatively, they can be slightly under-cooked, drained, tossed in butter, cooled quickly, packed and frozen, and are then best heated by plunging the freezing bag in boiling water, removing from heat and leaving 10 minutes.

Mashed potato with butter and hot milk can be frozen in bags or waxed cartons, and is best reheated in a double boiler, or can be used as a topping for meat or fish cooked in the oven. The same mixture made into croquettes and fried can be frozen in polythene bags. They should be thawed for 2 hours before heating in a moderate oven (350°F. or Gas Mark 4) for 20 minutes. Chips should be cooked in clean odour-free fat, drained on paper, cooled and frozen in bags. They can be re-heated on a baking tray in a low oven (300°F. or Gas Mark 2) for 12 minutes, sprinkled with salt. Alternatively, they may be heated in a frying pan with a little hot fat.

Baked potatoes can be frozen if the pulp is scooped out and mashed with milk, butter and seasoning, then returned to the shells, wrapped in foil or freezer paper and frozen. They are reheated in a moderate oven (350°F. or Gas Mark 4) in foil until steaming.

Mashed, fried and baked potatoes should be stored no longer than 3 months.

PUMPKIN

Prepare as cooked Marrow. Use as a vegetable, or for pie filling.

SPINACH

Choose young tender spinach without heavy leaf ribs. Remove stems and any bruised or discoloured leaves. Wash very thoroughly. Blanch for 2 minutes, moving the

Preparing pastry for the freezer: Foil dishes for baking pies. Ready-made pastry. Baked and unbaked pies to go in polythene.

Ready for freezing: Pies. Crumpets. Chips. Sponge cake. Cauliflower. Pigeons. Chocolate cake. Raspberries. Ice Cream. Sliced meat in sauce. Vegetable puree.

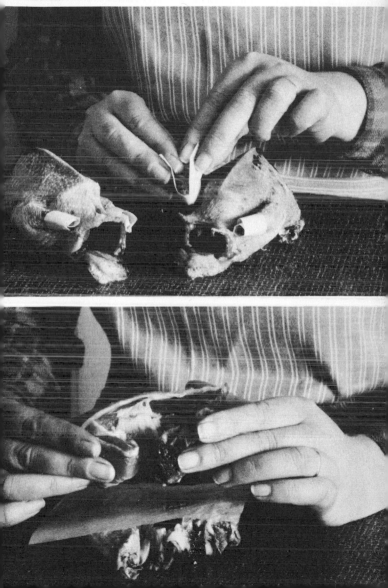

Top: Wrapping sharp bones on pigeons to prevent punctured wrappings

Bottom: Dividing chops with paper, for easy separations, before wrapping

Top: Freezing pigeons: Begin with wrapping birds in polythene sheeting after padding bones (see previous page) same process applies to freezer paper

Bottom: Completing the wrapping of pigeons in polythene to form parcel shape

Right: Sealing folds on parcel with special deep-freeze tape

Extracting air from polythene bag with a drinking straw

Cooling cauliflower sprigs after blanching, using deep-fry basket

Top: Packing cauliflower sprigs into rigid container

Bottom: Sealing the join between lid and base of rigid container

Swedish freezer boxes specially designed for stacking: 15, 30, 35 and 75 fl. oz. capacity. From Frigicold

Rigid containers, foil, gusseted polythene bag, waxed cartons, tubs with flush and screw lids, boxes with tuck-in and fitted lids. From Frigicold

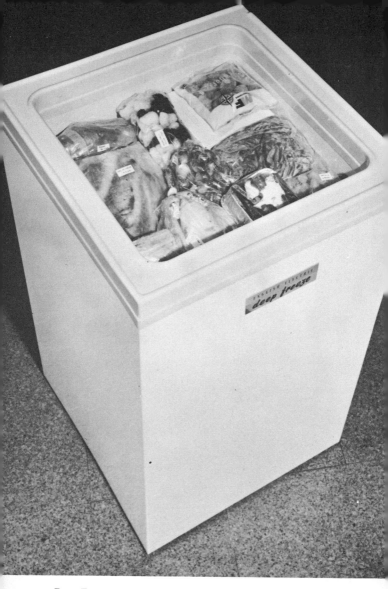

Deep Freeze cabinet in white enamel with plastic lid. 4.05 cubic ft. capacity. Will store approx. 124 lbs. of food. English Electric

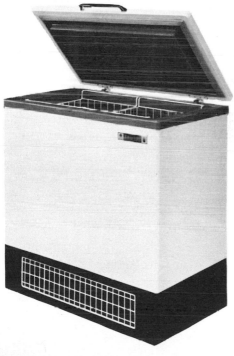

Above:
Chest Freezer designed with minimum width for narrow doors or stairs. Two sizes: 6.2 and 9.5 cu. ft. capacity. Total Refrigeration Ltd.

Left:
Chest Freezer with sealed refrigerating system giving high efficiency with low running costs. Swivel castors for easy moving. Prestcold

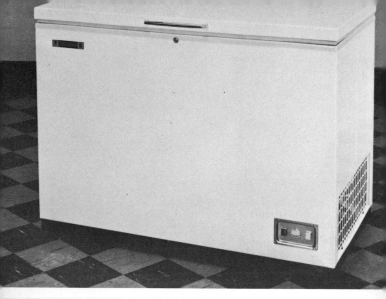

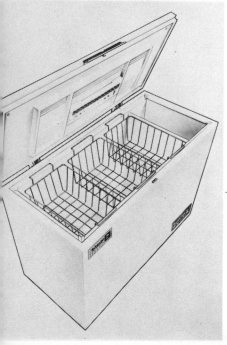

Above:
Chest freezer
giving maximum
capacity within
minimum cabinet
dimensions.
16 cu. ft. holds
approx. 500 lbs
food. Prestcold

Left:
Chest freezer with
fast-freezing shelf.
10 cu. ft. size holds
350 lbs food and
15 cu. ft. holds
524 lbs food.
Kelvinator

Top Right:
Upright freezer
with shelves and
fitted door space.
4 cu. ft. with left
or right hand
hinged doors.
Kelvinator

Bottom Right:
Upright freezer
to be used on a
shelf, work-top
or fitted to
any refrigerator
in manufacturer's
range. 1.75 cu. ft.
holds 60 lbs food.
Hoover

Above: Combined
Refrigerator-freezer. 23″
wide by 25¾″ deep. Holds
130 lbs. of food. Electrolux
Helifrost by Helimatic.

Right: Two-door
refrigerator-freezer.
Two sizes: 6.7 cu. ft. holds
approx 45 lbs food.
8.2 cu. ft. holds approx
63 lbs food. Philips
Electrical

Slimly designed refrigerator-freezer. Refrigerator: 4.1 cu. ft. with freezer 1.4. cu. ft. Suitable for small kitchens. English Electric

Refrigerator-freezer with freezer at the bottom. Both sections have a 6 cu. ft. capacity. Total Refrigeration Ltd.

container so the leaves separate. Cool quickly and press out excess moisture with a wooden spoon. Pack in rigid containers, leaving $\frac{1}{2}$ inch headspace, or in polythene bags. To serve, cook 7 minutes in a little melted butter. Storage time: 1 year.

TOMATOES
Tomatoes cannot be successfully frozen for salad use, but are useful for cooking. Whole tomatoes should be wiped clean, and stems removed before packing in polythene bags. Storage time: 10–12 months. They should be thawed for 2 hours at room temperature before using.

Tomato pulp is very useful for cooking. It is best to prepare this by putting tomatoes in boiling water till skins crack, then removing skins and cores and simmering tomatoes in their own juice for 5 minutes until soft. Put through a sieve, cool and pack in cartons. Storage time: 1 year.

Tomato juice is easily made by coring and quartering ripe tomatoes, and simmering them covered for 10 minutes. Put through muslin, cool and pack into cartons, leaving 1 inch headspace. Thaw juice in containers in refrigerator, and season with salt, pepper and a squeeze of lemon juice.

TURNIPS
Use only small, young mild-flavoured turnips. Trim and peel them, and cut into $\frac{1}{2}$ inch dice. Blanch for $2\frac{1}{2}$ minutes, cool and pack in rigid containers. Serve by cooking 10 minutes in boiling water. Storage time: 1 year. Mashed turnips may also be prepared by cooking until tender, draining, mashing and freezing in rigid containers leaving $\frac{1}{2}$ inch headspace.

VEGETABLE PUREE
It is particularly useful to freeze vegetables as puree for soups and for baby food. The vegetable should be cooked until tender, drained and sieved and chilled rapidly before packing into rigid containers leaving $\frac{1}{2}$ inch head-

81

space. Small quantities of puree may be frozen in ice cube trays, each cube being wrapped in foil and packaged in quantities in polythene bags for storage. One cube will provide a serving for a baby. Puree is best reheated in a double boiler.

MIXED VEGETABLES
Vegetables such as peas, beans, carrots and corn may be mixed in freezer packs. Each vegetable should be prepared and blanched separately, then mixed for packing.

COOKED VEGETABLE DISHES
It is possible to freeze cooked vegetables in a variety of sauces e.g. cauliflower, celery, carrots in white sauce, or onions in gravy, but preparation must be very accurate to avoid overcooking since the dish will be reheated to serve. There is a possibility of producing a dish with poor texture and colour and a warmed-up flavour. In view of the time taken to reheat the dish, better results are obtained by freezing vegetables after blanching, with the sauces frozen separately, and combining the two items as required for serving.

If vegetables in sauces are wanted in the freezer, the vegetables should be slightly undercooked, and the prepared dish cooled as quickly as possible before freezing. The frozen item can be reheated in a double pan or slow oven, or if packed in a moisture-vapour-proof bag, this can be immersed in boiling water for 20 minutes. A pinch of monosodium glutinate in these prepared dishes will improve flavour.

Chapter 14

FRUIT

Fruit is perhaps the most useful out-of-season item to be stored in the freezer. Freezing is suitable for all types of fruit, unlike bottling and canning, and can also be used for preserving juices and syrups. This means that as well as garden produce, imported fruits such as pineapples, avocados and figs can be frozen when they are plentiful and cheap.

Best results are from fully flavoured fruits, particularly berries. The blander fruits such as pears are satisfactory, but have little flavour. In general, fruit for freezing should be first quality; over-ripe fruit will be mushy (though it may be possible to store as puree); unripe fruit will be tasteless and poorly-coloured.

It is important to work quickly when preparing fruit; home-picked fruit should be frozen on the same day, while fruit from shop or market should only be bought in manageable quantities which can be handled in a short space of time.

Whichever method of packing is to be used, wash the fruit in plenty of water containing ice cubes as this will prevent the fruit becoming soggy and losing juice. Fruit should be drained immediately (avoid copper, iron and galvanised ware which produce off-flavours) in enamel, aluminium, stainless steel or earthenware, and may be further drained on absorbent paper. It is important to be gentle in removing stems or stones from fruit to be frozen; this should be done with the tips of the fingers, without squeezing.

There are four ways of packing fruit for freezing:

UNSWEETENED DRY PACK
This pack can be used for fruit which it is intended to use for pies, puddings and jams, or for people on a sugar-

free diet. It should not be used for fruit which discolours badly during preparation, as sugar helps to retard the action of the enzymes which cause darkening.

To pack fruit by this method, wash and drain and pack into cartons. Seal and freeze and label carefully.

UNSWEETENED WET PACK

This method is little used, but is acceptable for very sweet fruit or for those puddings which may be made for people on a diet. The fruit should be packed in liquid-proof containers, either gently crushed in its own juice, or covered with water to which lemon juice has been added to prevent discolouration (juice of 1 lemon to $1\frac{1}{2}$ pints water). If the fruit is tart but no sugar is to be used, it may be frozen in water sweetened with a sugar substitute, or with a sugar-free carbonated beverage. Seal and freeze and label carefully.

DRY SUGAR PACK

This is a good method for crushed or sliced fruit, or for soft juicy fruit from which the juice draws easily such as berries. The fruit should be washed and drained and may be packed by two methods: (a) mix fruit and sugar in a bowl with a silver spoon, adjusting sweetening to tartness of fruit (average 3 pounds fruit to 1 pound sugar). Pack fruit into containers, leaving $\frac{1}{2}$ inch headspace, seal and freeze, labelling carefully: (b) pack fruit in layers, using same proportion of fruit and sugar; start with a layer of fruit, sprinkle with sugar, then more fruit and sugar, leaving $\frac{1}{2}$ inch headspace, sealing and freezing, labelling carefully.

SYRUP PACK

This method is best for non-juicy fruits and those which discolour easily. Syrup is normally made from white sugar and water. For those who dislike white sugar for dietary reasons, honey may be used, but flavours the fruit strongly. Brown sugar may be used, but affects the colour of the fruit.

The type of syrup to be used is referred to in a percentage, according to the amount of sugar and water used. A medium syrup or 40% syrup is best for most purposes as a heavier syrup tends to make the fruit flabby. Use a breakfast cup to measure quantities. The sugar must be completely dissolved in boiling water, then cooled. It must be completely cold before adding to the fruit, and is best stored in a refrigerator for a day before using. The fruit should be packed into containers and covered with syrup, leaving ½ to 1 inch headspace. To prevent discolouration, a piece of Cellophane should be pressed down over the fruit into the syrup before sealing, freezing and labelling.

SYRUP

Sugar	Water	Type of Syrup	Yield
1 CUP	4 CUPS	20% VERY LIGHT SYRUP	5 CUPS
2 CUPS	4 CUPS	30% LIGHT SYRUP	5⅛ CUPS
3½ CUPS	4 CUPS	40% MEDIUM SYRUP	5½ CUPS
4¾ CUPS	4 CUPS	50% HEAVY SYRUP	6½ CUPS
7 CUPS	4 CUPS	60% VERY HEAVY SYRUP	7¼ CUPS
9 CUPS	4 CUPS	70% EXTRA HEAVY SYRUP	8⅝ CUPS

HEADSPACE

Headspace must be allowed for all fruit in sugar or syrup, for juice or puree: ½ inch should be allowed for all dry packs; ½ to 1 inch per pint for wide-topped wet packs, and ¾ to 1 inch per pint for narrow-topped wet packs. Double headspace is needed for quart containers.

DISCOLOURATION

Discolouration is the greatest problem in fruit packing for freezing. Apples, peaches and pears are particularly subject to this during preparation, storage and thawing. In general, fruit which has a lot of Vitamin C darkens less easily, so the addition of lemon juice or citric acid to the sugar pack will help to arrest darkening (use the juice of 1 lemon to 1½ pints water, or 1 teaspoon citric acid to each 1 pound of sugar in dry pack). Fruit puree in particular is subject to darkening since large amounts of air are forced through a sieve during preparation. Air reacts on the cells of fruit to produce darkening, and for this reason fruit should be prepared quickly for freezing once the natural protection of skin or rind is broken. For the same reason, fruit should be eaten immediately on thawing, or while a few ice crystals remain. Fruit which discolours badly is better for rapid thawing, and unsweetened frozen fruit should be put at once into hot syrup.

STORAGE TIME
Most fruits, puree and juices can be stored up to a year. Pre-cooked fruit should be used within 4 months.

LABELLING
Since there are so many different ways in which fruit can be packed, labelling is particularly important. Not only should the label state the type of fruit, but also whether it is preserved whole, in slices or in puree, whether it is suitable for serving immediately, or is for pies or jam. Finally the type of pack should be noted i.e. unsweetened dry, unsweetened wet, dry sugar or syrup.

FRUIT PUREE
It is useful to freeze puree for certain kinds of puddings, and when there is a lot of ripe fruit. The fruit should not be over-ripe or bruised. Raw fruit such as raspberries or strawberries should be sieved, with all pips excluded. Other fruit can be put in a covered dish in the oven to start the juice running before the fruit is sieved. Puree may be made from cooked fruit and must be cooled before freezing (it will keep less than 4 months). The puree should be sweetened as one would wish for immediate use. Ways of preparing puree from individual fruits are given under the fruit names.

FRUIT SYRUPS

Fruit syrups can be frozen; the best type is blackcurrant, and it is far easier to freeze than to bottle. Any standard syrup recipe can be used and it is best frozen in small quantities in ice-cube trays. Each cube can be wrapped in foil, and then a number packed into a bag for storage. One syrup cube will give an individual serving to use with puddings or ice cream, or to dissolve in water as a drink.

FRUIT JUICES

Ripe fruit may be turned into juice and frozen in this form. Citrus fruit juice may also be frozen. Non-citrus fruit should be carefully checked for any bruising or insects, then mashed with a silver fork. For each 4 cups of fruit, allow 1 cup of water and simmer gently for 10 minutes. Strain through a jelly bag or cloth, and cool completely before freezing. These juices may be frozen unsweetened, or sweetened to taste, and are useful for drinks, jellies and fruit pies. Freeze them in a rigid container, leaving ½ inch headspace, or in ice-cube trays, wrapping each cube in foil and storing in quantities in polythene bags. Apple juice can be made, using ½ pint water to each 2 pounds apples, or it can be made by simmering leftover peelings in water; it should not be sweetened before freezing as fermentation sets in quickly.

Citrus fruit juices can easily be prepared from good quality fruit which is heavy in the hand for its size. The unpeeled fruit should be chilled in ice water or in the refrigerator before the juice is extracted; the juice may be strained or the fine pulp left in if preferred. Freeze in rigid containers, leaving 1 inch headspace. Lemon and lime juice can usefully be frozen in ice-cube trays, each cube being wrapped in foil and stored in quantity in a polythene bag.

CATERING PACKS OF FRUIT AND JUICE

Large tins of fruit in syrup and of fruit juices may be bought economically. They can be opened and divided into normal family portions and frozen in smaller containers.

THAWING FROZEN FRUIT

Unsweetened fruit packs take longer to thaw than sweetened ones; fruit in dry sugar thaws most quickly of all. All fruit should be thawed in its unopened container, and fruit is at its best just thawed with a few ice crystals left if it is to be eaten raw. Fruit to use with ice cream should only be partly defrosted. To cook frozen fruit, thaw until pieces can just be separated and put into a pie; if fruit is to be cooked in a saucepan, it can be put into the pan in its frozen state, keeping in mind the amount of sugar or syrup used in freezing when a pudding is being made. Frozen fruits are likely to have a lot of juice after thawing; to avoid leaky pies or damp cake fillings, add a little thickening for pies (such as cornflour, arrowroot or flake tapioca), or drain off excess juice.

For each 1 pound fruit packed in syrup, allow 6–8 hours thawing time in the refrigerator, 2–4 hours thawing time at room temperature, and $\frac{1}{2}$–1 hour if the pack is placed in a bowl of cold water.

Fruit will lose quality and flavour if left to stand for any length of time after thawing, so it is best not to thaw more than needed immediately. If leftover fruit is cooked, it will last several days in a refrigerator.

APPLES

Choose crisp firm apples for freezing, particularly for pie slices. Apples which burst and "fluff" in cooking are good to freeze as puree or apple sauce.

For pies or puddings, peel and core apples and drop them into a basin of cold water. Slice medium-sized apples into twelfths, large ones into sixteenths. Apples are best packed with sugar. For a dry sugar pack, use a proportion of $\frac{1}{2}$ pound sugar to 2 pounds fruit, and leave $\frac{1}{2}$ inch headspace. For syrup pack, use 40% syrup, quarter-filling pack with syrup and slicing apples into containers, finishing with more syrup if necessary, covering with Cellophane, and leaving $\frac{1}{2}$ inch headspace.

Apple slices may also be blanched for 3 minutes and cooled quickly before packing.

For baked apples, use large firm fruit and wash apples well. Remove core, leaving $\frac{1}{4}$ inch at bottom to hold filling. Fill with brown sugar, preferred spice and a squeeze of lemon juice and bake at 400°F. until apples are tender. Cool. Pack apples into individual waxed tubs or foil dishes (in larger dishes, apples may be separated by Cellophane). Cover and freeze. These apples may be eaten cold or heated.

For apple sauce, cook apples to a pulp with a minimum of water. This is best done in a casserole in the oven, and flavour will be better if the apples are cooked sliced but unpeeled. Sieve the sauce and sweeten to taste, adding a squeeze of lemon juice. Cool and pack, leaving $\frac{1}{2}$ inch headspace. Thawing time: 3 hours at room temperature. Storage time: 1 year.

APRICOTS

Apricots may be frozen in halves without peeling, or in peeled slices for use fresh or cooked. Very ripe fruit may be frozen as puree to serve as a sauce or for making ice-cream. Use small quantities to avoid discolouration. If apricots are to be left unpeeled, dropping the halves into boiling water for $\frac{1}{2}$ minute will stop the skins toughening in the freezer.

To freeze half apricots, wash them under cold running water, cut into halves and remove stones, and drop into boiling water for $\frac{1}{2}$ minute. Chill in ice water and drain. Pack in dry sugar, using 4 ounces sugar to each pound of fruit, or use 40% syrup.

To freeze slices, peel apricots quickly, then slice directly into container quarter-full of 40% syrup. Top up with syrup to keep fruit covered, put Cellophane on top, allow $\frac{1}{2}$ inch headspace. Thawing time: $3\frac{1}{4}$ hours at room temperature. Storage time: 1 year.

AVOCADO PEARS

The subtlety of flavour of this fruit is lost in freezing

and the flesh discolours very quickly when cut. It is possible to halve the fruit, removing the stone, rub each cut side with lemon juice, wrap each piece in foil, then put the fruit into polythene bags for freezing. Slices can also be dipped in lemon juice and frozen, to use in salads. The best use of ripe avocados in freezing is to keep the mashed pulp to use for savoury dips and spreads. Fully ripe avocado pears should be scooped out and mashed, and 1 tablespoon lemon juice blended in with each avocado. Put the mashed pulp into small containers and freeze. To use, mix the mashed pulp with onion, garlic or herbs. Thawing time: $2\frac{1}{2}$–3 hours at room temperature. Storage time: 3 months.

BANANAS
It seems unlikely one would ever need to freeze bananas, but it can be done, and the pulp used in making bread and cakes and in sandwiches. The fruit discolours very rapidly and should be mashed in a chilled bowl, then mixed with 8 ounces sugar to 3 breakfast cups banana pulp and 3 tablespoons lemon juice. Pack in small quantities which can be used very quickly. Defrost unopened in a refrigerator until soft enough to work with. Thawing time: 3 to $3\frac{1}{2}$ hours at room temperature. Storage time: 2 months.

BLACKBERRIES
Use fully ripe blackberries that are dark and glossy, avoiding those with woody pips, or any which have green patches. Wash in small quantities in ice-chilled water and drain almost dry in absorbent paper. Pack dry and un-sweetened, or in dry sugar (8 ounces sugar to 2 pounds fruit) or in 50% syrup, leaving headspace. Crushed berries can be sieved and sweetened, allowing 4 ounces sugar to 1 pint of crushed berries, stirred until dissolved, and packed leaving $\frac{1}{2}$ inch headspace. Thawing time: 3 hours at room temperature. Storage time: 1 year.

BLUEBERRIES

The skin of these berries tends to toughen on freezing and it is best to crush them slightly before freezing. Alternatively, the berries may be held over steam for 1 minute, then cooled before packaging. The berries should be washed in ice-chilled water and drained thoroughly. They may be packed unsweetened and dry if they are to be cooked later; if to be served uncooked, use 50% syrup. If a dry sugar pack is preferred, crush fruit slightly and mix well with sugar (4 ounces sugar to 4 breakfastcups berries) until sugar is dissolved. Thawing time: 3 hours at room temperature. Storage time: 1 year.

CHERRIES

Sweet and sour cherries may be frozen, but red varieties are better than black for processing. The cherries should be firmed in ice-chilled water for 1 hour before processing, then thoroughly dried and stones removed as these may flavour fruit during storage. Use glass or plastic containers as the acid in cherry juice tends to remain liquid during freezing and may leak through cardboard. Cherries for pie-making are best in a dry sugar pack, allowing ½ pound sugar to 2 pounds pitted cherries. For sweet cherries, a 40% syrup is best, and for sour cherries 50% or 60% syrup depending on tartness, if this method of packing is preferred. Thawing time: 3 hours at room temperature. Storage time: 1 year.

COCONUT

It is rare to find really fresh coconuts in Britain, but if they can be tracked down, the frozen shredded flesh is delicious for use in fruit salads and icings, and for curry dishes. Choose coconuts which contain milk and drain off this milk. Grate or shred the coconut, moisten with the coconut milk and pack into bags or containers. If to be used for sweet dishes, 4 ounces sugar may be added to 4 breakfastcups of shredded coconut. Thawing time: 2 hours at room temperature. Storage time: 6 months.

CRABAPPLES
If there is no time to make crabapple jelly at the appropriate season, the fruit may be frozen in the same way as apples in slices.

CRANBERRIES
Cranberries for freezing should be firm, well-coloured and glossy, without mealiness. They should be carefully sorted, omitting any shrivelled or soft berries, washed in cold water and drained. As they will most likely be converted into sauce at a later date, they are best packed dry and unsweetened in bags or containers. If puree is preferred, cook berries gently in very little water until the skins pop; put through a sieve and add sugar to taste (about 8 ounces sugar to each pint of puree). Pack into containers, allowing $\frac{1}{2}$ inch headspace. Thawing time: $3\frac{1}{2}$ hours at room temperature. Storage time: 1 year.

CURRANTS
Black, red and white currants are all frozen in the same way. They should be stripped from the stem with a fork and washed in ice-chilled water, then dried gently. For later use in jam-making, pack dry into polythene bags. For a dry sugar pack, use 8 ounces sugar to 1 pound prepared berries, mixing until most of the sugar is dissolved. Use 40% syrup for this pack if preferred. Thawing time: $\frac{3}{4}$ hour at room temperature. Storage time: 1 year. *Boskoop Giant* and *Wellington* are good blackcurrant varieties for freezing.

DAMSONS
Damsons tend to acquire a tough skin during freezing, and the stones can flavour the fruit, and it is therefore

worth taking the trouble to freeze them in puree form. If a syrup pack is preferred, wash fruit in ice-chilled water, cut in half and take out stones, then pack in 50% syrup. Thawing time: 2½ hours at room temperature. Storage time: 1 year.

DATES
Dates stored in boxes tend to dry out and acquire off-flavours. When good quality fruit is available, remove stones and freeze in polythene bags. The fruit is delicious eaten straight from the freezer or may be used for cakes and puddings.

FIGS
Green and purple figs may be successfully frozen. Choose fully-ripe figs which are soft and sweet with small seeds and slightly shrivelled but unsplit skins. Wash in ice-chilled water and remove stems with a sharp knife; handle carefully as figs bruise easily. They may be frozen whole and unpeeled or peeled. The easiest method is to freeze them whole and unsweetened in polythene bags. For dessert use, they are delicious peeled and frozen in 30% syrup. Thawing time: 1½ hours at room temperature. Storage time: 1 year.

GOOSEBERRIES
These may be frozen in a variety of ways according to the use to which they will be put on thawing. They should be washed in ice-chilled water and dried. For pies, they should be frozen when fully ripe in bags or containers without sweetening. For jam-making, the fruit can be frozen slightly under-ripe. Puree can be made by stewing the fruit in very little water, sieving and sweetening to taste, and this is useful at a later date for fools. Thawing time: 2½ hours at room temperature. Storage time: 1 year. *Careless* is an excellent variety for freezing.

GRAPEFRUIT
This is a nuisance to prepare, but very worth while for

breakfast use. Peel fruit, remove all pith and cut segments away from pith. Pack dry with sugar (8 ounces sugar to 2 breakfast cups segments) or pack in 50% syrup. Thawing time: 2½ hours at room temperature. Storage time: 1 year.

GRAPES

Choose firm, ripe grapes which are sweet and have tender skins. The seedless varieties can be packed whole, but others should be skinned and pipped and cut in half. They are best packed in 30% syrup. Thawing time: 2½ hours at room temperature. Storage time: 1 year. A really perfect bunch of grapes can be frozen, perhaps as a centrepiece for a dinner table dessert bowl, and can be kept for 2 weeks by this method; just put the whole bunch into a polythene bag to freeze. The frozen grapes look full and rich for decorative purposes but are also good to eat treated in this way.

GREENGAGES

Wash fruit in ice-chilled water and dry well. Cut in halves, removing stones, and pack in 40% syrup. As with all stone fruit, the stone tends to flavour the fruit during freezing, and the skins may toughen, so that an unsweetened dry pack is not recommended.

LEMONS AND LIMES

Peeled lemon or lime slices may be frozen to be used as garnishes or in drinks. They are best frozen in 20% syrup. Thawing time: 1 hour at room temperature for small packs. Storage time: 1 year.

LOGANBERRIES

Follow directions for preparing and freezing Blackberries.

MELONS

All varieties of melon can be frozen, though watermelon is a little difficult to prepare because of the seeds distributed through the flesh. Cut flesh in cubes or balls and toss in lemon juice before packing in 30% syrup. Do not allow melon to thaw completely, but defrost unopened in refrigerator, and serve while still a little frosty. Thawing time: 3 hours in refrigerator. Storage time 1 year.

NECTARINES
Follow directions for preparing and freezing Peaches.

ORANGES
Sweet oranges can be frozen in sections (see Grapefruit), but pack better if frozen in slices, which is also more useful for serving at meals other than breakfast. Peel fruit and remove all pith. Cut into $\frac{1}{4}$ inch slices and pack in 30% syrup. Fruit may also be packed in dry sugar (8 ounces sugar to 3 breakfastcups orange pieces), or is delicious packed in the juice of squeezed oranges sweetened to taste.

PEACHES
Peaches must be prepared with great care as they discolour quickly. They should be peeled, halved and stoned, then brushed with lemon juice to stop colouring. Only prepare one peach at a time. Peaches may be halved or sliced, and are best packed in 40% syrup. To prevent browning and softness, it is better, though more trouble, to peel and stone peaches under cold running water rather than dipping them in boiling water to aid the removal of skin. Since peaches begin to discolour as soon as they are exposed to the air, it is better to defrost them slowly in a refrigerator and serve while still a little frosty. If they are to be used in cakes or topped with cream, they can be used half-thawed, put into the appropriate dish and will be ready for eating by the time preparation is finished. Peach puree may be made for use as a sauce or for making into ice-cream. The peaches should be peeled and stoned, crushed with a silver fork, and mixed with 1 tablespoon lemon juice and 4 ounces sugar to each pound of fruit, before packing into

95

containers. Thawing time: 3 hours in a refrigerator. Storage time: 1 year.

PEARS
Pears do not freeze very well owing to their delicate flavour, and the fact that their flesh does not keep its paleness. Choose ripe, but not over-ripe pears with strong flavour. Peel and quarter them, remove cores and dip pieces in lemon juice immediately. Make up 30% syrup and poach pears in this for $1\frac{1}{2}$ minutes. Drain and cool and pack into cold 30% syrup. Thawing time: 3 hours at room temperature. Storage time: 1 year.

PINEAPPLE
Pineapple freezes very well indeed, if the fruit is ripe, with golden yellow flesh. Peel the fruit and cut into slices or chunks. Freeze in dry unsweetened packs, using double thickness of Cellophane to keep slices separate. Pineapple may also be frozen in 30% syrup including any pineapple juice which has resulted from the preparation. Crushed pineapple can be packed with sugar, using 4 ounces sugar to each 2 breakfast cups of prepared fruit. Thawing time: 3 hours at room temperature. Storage time: 1 year.

PLUMS
Follow directions for preparing and freezing Greengages.

QUINCES
The flavour of quinces is retained beautifully in the freezer. Wash the quinces thoroughly, peel and remove cores. Put peelings (but not cores) into a pan with water to cover and the juice of 1 orange and 1 lemon. Simmer until peel is tender, then strain liquid over sliced quinces. Simmer quinces in this juice until just tender, then remove from heat and stir in $1\frac{1}{2}$ pounds sugar (to each 2 pounds prepared quinces) until dissolved. Cool, then strain off syrup and chill. Pack quince slices into containers, pour over syrup and cover, leaving $\frac{1}{2}$ inch head-

space. Thawing time: 3 hours at room temperature. Storage time: 1 year.

RASPBERRIES
Raspberries should be picked over very carefully, discarding any hard or seedy ones, then washed in ice-chilled water and dried very carefully. Freeze dry in cartons, or with sugar, allowing 4 ounces sugar to 1 pound raspberries. They may also be packed in 30% syrup. Raspberry puree is useful for a sauce and as a basis for fruit drinks and milk shakes. The berries should be put through a sieve and sweetened with 4 ounces sugar to each pint of puree. When the sugar is dissolved, the puree may be packed in containers or in ice cubes, and the frozen cubes wrapped in foil and packaged in quantities in polythene bags. Thawing time: 3 hours at room temperature. Storage time: 1 year. Best varieties for freezing are *Norfolk Giant* and *Lloyd George*.

RHUBARB
The early crop of young pink sticks is best for freezing. Sticks may be frozen unsweetened for pies after washing in cold running water and trimming to the desired length. They can be packed in cartons or in polythene bags or in foil. To make packing easier, stalks may be blanched for 1 minute, which makes them slightly limp and easier to pack, and colour and flavour will also be better by this method. The fruit may also be packed in 40% syrup, or stewed rhubarb can be sieved and sweetened and frozen as puree. Thawing time: 3½ hours at room temperature. Storage time: 1 year.

STRAWBERRIES
Strawberries are best frozen dry, when they tend to be less pulpy on thawing. Husks should be removed from berries which are fully ripe and mature, but firm. The most satisfactory way to freeze strawberries is to slice them or slightly crush them if a sugar or syrup pack is preferred. For a dry sugar pack, use 4 ounces sugar to

each pound of fruit. Use 40% syrup for this type of pack. Ripe strawberries which have been sieved and sweetened to taste may be frozen as puree, and make a delicious strawberry ice served in the frozen state. Thawing time: 1½ hours at room temperature. Storage time: 1 year. The best varieties for freezing are *Cambridge Vigour*, *Cambridge Favourite*, and *Royal Sovereign*.

Chapter 15

SOUPS AND SAUCES

Soups and sauces are two of the most useful freezer items to be prepared in advance, then quickly heated for complete meals. Both take a lot of cooking time, so they are invaluable stored against the days when there is little time to prepare food but nourishing meals are needed. The preparation of soups and sauces is also one of the most useful ways of practising kitchen economy, for stock can be kept safely, and vegetables can be preserved in a handy form when they are at their cheapest.

SOUP
Soup containing ordinary flour tends to curdle on reheating, so cornflour is best used as a thickening agent. Rice flour may be used but gives a glutinous result; porridge oats may be used for the thicker meat soups, but does not give the creamy result of cornflour.

A certain amount of experiment is needed to find the most satisfactory soups for storage. Those containing milk and cream give varying results, and it is better to prepare stocks or purées which can be frozen well and added to in the final heating. Starchy foods such as rice, pasta, barley or potatoes are not satisfactory when frozen in soup, and should also be added in the final heating.

When preparing soup, it should be cooled and all surplus fat removed as this will separate in storage. Soup should be frozen in water-tight containers with a headspace of ½ inch for wide-topped containers and ¾ inch for narrow-topped containers. Soup should not be stored for more than 2 months, and it is worth remembering that it will thicken during storage, and is better seasoned on thawing.

Rigid plastic containers are very useful for storing soup, but if space is at a premium, large quantities may be frozen in bread tins or freezer boxes lined with foil. When a block is solid, it can be wrapped in foil and stored like a brick.

Clear soups can be heated over a low flame, but cream soups should be heated in a double boiler and well beaten to keep them smooth.

SAUCES

Both sweet and savoury sauces can be frozen. They may be in the form of complete sauces for use with spaghetti or rice for instance, or can be basic sauces such as white or brown to be used with other ingredients on reheating. Mayonnaise and custard sauces cannot be frozen as the ingredients freeze at different temperatures and give unsatisfactory results.

Sauces give the same problem as soups, in that they are liable to curdling if made with flour, and cornflour is the best thickening agent.

Like soups, sauces may be stored in large quantities in waterproof containers, or in "brick" form, but where small quantities are required, these may be frozen in ice cube trays, then wrapped individually in foil and packed in quantities in bags for easy storage. Flavoured butters can also be usefully stored for use with meat and fish. The butter should be prepared with flavourings (see recipe for Parsley Butter), formed into a roll, wrapped in greaseproof paper and polythene and frozen; slices can be quickly cut off to serve at a meal.

MEAT STOCK

I POUND SHIN BEEF	I SMALL ONION
(INCLUDING BONES)	PARSLEY AND BAYLEAF
I QUART WATER	6 PEPPERCORNS
I CARROT	$\frac{1}{2}$ TEASPOON SALT

Put meat and bones into water, cover and simmer for 2 hours. Cut vegetables in small pieces, fry lightly and add to liquid together with seasoning. Simmer for 2 hours, strain and cool. Remove fat and put into cartons, seal, label and freeze. Thaw in saucepan over low heat.

CHICKEN STOCK

1 CHICKEN CARCASS

1 QUART WATER

1 CARROT

1 ONION

1 STICK CELERY

SPRIG OF PARSLEY

PINCH OF SALT

Break up carcass and put in pan with sliced vegetables, water and salt. Simmer for 2 hours, strain and cool. Remove fat from surface. Put into cartons, seal, label and freeze. Thaw in saucepan over low heat.

TOMATO SOUP

2 POUNDS TOMATOES

2 OUNCES MUSHROOMS

2 MEDIUM ONIONS

1 LEEK

2 STICKS CELERY

JUICE OF 1 LEMON

PARSLEY, THYME, BAYLEAF

2 OUNCES BUTTER

3 PINTS STOCK

2 OUNCES RICE FLOUR

2 EGG YOLKS

$\frac{1}{4}$ PINT CREAMY MILK

PINCH OF SUGAR

SALT AND PEPPER

RED COLOURING

Slice tomatoes. Slice mushrooms, onions, leek and celery and fry lightly in butter. Add lemon juice, herbs and stock, and tomatoes, and simmer for 30 minutes. Put through a sieve. Mix egg yolks, rice flour and milk until creamy and add a little hot mixture, stirring gently. Add to remaining liquid and cook very gently for 10 minutes without boiling. Season to taste with sugar, salt and pepper and colour lightly if necessary. Cool, pour into cartons, seal, label and freeze. Reheat in a double boiler, stirring gently.

OXTAIL SOUP

1 OXTAIL

2½ PINTS WATER

2 CARROTS

2 MEDIUM ONIONS

1 TURNIP

1 STICK CELERY

PINCH OF SALT

Cut oxtail in small pieces and wipe clean. Toss in a little seasoned flour and fry in a little butter for 10 minutes. Put in saucepan with water and simmer 2 hours. Remove meat from bones and return to stock with cut up vegetables. Simmer $\frac{3}{4}$ hour and sieve or liquidise. Cool and remove any fat. Put into containers, seal, label and freeze. Reheat gently in saucepan, seasoning with $\frac{1}{2}$ teaspoon Worcester sauce and $\frac{1}{2}$ teaspoon lemon juice (write these additions on the freezer label).

SCOTCH BROTH

1 POUND LEAN NECK OF	1 ONION
MUTTON	1 CARROT
4 PINTS WATER	1 TURNIP
1 LEEK	SPRIG OF PARSLEY
2 STICKS OF CELERY	PEPPER AND SALT

Cut meat into neat squares and simmer with water for 1 hour. Add diced vegetables and seasoning and continue cooking for $1\frac{1}{2}$ hours. Cool and remove fat, and take out parsley. Pour into containers, seal, label and freeze. Reheat gently in saucepan, adding 2 tablespoons barley and cook until barley is tender.

KIDNEY SOUP

8 OUNCES OX KIDNEY	1 CARROT
1 OUNCE BUTTER	PARSLEY, THYME, BAYLEAF
1 SMALL ONION	SALT AND PEPPER
1 QUART STOCK	1 OUNCE CORNFLOUR

Wash and dry kidney and cut in slices, and slice onion. Cook until onion is soft and golden. Add stock, chopped vegetables and herbs and seasoning and simmer for $1\frac{1}{2}$ hours. Sieve and return to pan. Thicken with cornflour and cook 5 minutes. Cool, put into containers, seal, label and freeze. Thaw in double boiler, adding $\frac{1}{2}$ gill sherry if liked.

BROWN VEGETABLE SOUP

2 CARROTS	PARSLEY, THYME, BAYLEAF
2 TURNIPS	SALT AND PEPPER
2 ONIONS	1 OUNCE CORNFLOUR
1 QUART STOCK	

Cut carrots and turnips into rough pieces. Slice onions

and lightly brown them in a little dripping. Add stock and vegetables together with herbs and seasoning and simmer for 1 hour. Put through a sieve, thicken with cornflour, and simmer 5 minutes. Cool, put into containers, seal, label and freeze. Thaw in top of double boiler.

WHITE SAUCE

1 SMALL ONION	1 PINT MILK
1 CARROT	1 OUNCE CORNFLOUR
1 BAYLEAF	SALT AND PEPPER
1 OUNCE BUTTER	

Cut onion and carrot into slices and simmer with bayleaf in milk for 15 minutes. Melt butter in pan, work in cornflour and cook for 2 minutes, stirring carefully. Add milk gradually, beating thoroughly, and season to taste. Cool, put into containers, seal, label and freeze. Thaw in top of double boiler.

TOMATO SAUCE

1 POUND TOMATOES	1 PINT STOCK
1 OUNCE BUTTER	PARSLEY, THYME, BAYLEAF
1 SMALL ONION	$\frac{1}{2}$ OUNCE CORNFLOUR
1 SMALL CARROT	SALT AND PEPPER
1 OUNCE HAM	

Cut tomatoes in slices. Melt butter and fry sliced onion and carrot until golden. Add tomatoes, ham, stock, and herbs and simmer for 30 minutes. Put through a sieve, thicken with cornflour, season to taste, and cook for 5 minutes, stirring well. Cool, put into containers, seal, label and freeze. Thaw in top of double boiler.

SPAGHETTI SAUCE

1 LARGE CHOPPED ONION	6 OUNCES TOMATO PUREE
1 CLOVE GARLIC	$\frac{1}{2}$ PINT WATER
2 TABLESPOONS OLIVE OIL	1 TEASPOON SALT
1 POUND MINCED BEEF	$\frac{1}{2}$ TEASPOON PEPPER
1 POUND CHOPPED PEELED TOMATOES	1 BAYLEAF

Fry onion and crushed garlic in oil, add beef and cook until browned. Add all the other ingredients and simmer slowly for 1 hour until thick and well blended. Cool, put into containers, seal, label and freeze. Thaw gently over direct heat.

BREAD SAUCE

1 SMALL ONION	2 OUNCES BREADCRUMBS
4 CLOVES	½ OUNCE BUTTER
½ PINT MILK	SALT AND PEPPER

Peel onion and stick with cloves. Put all ingredients into saucepan and simmer for 1 hour. Remove onion, beat sauce well, and season further to taste. Cool, put into containers, seal, label and freeze. Thaw in top of double boiler, adding a little cream if liked.

PARSLEY BUTTER

2 OUNCES BUTTER	2 TEASPOONS CHOPPED
2 TEASPOONS LEMON JUICE	PARSLEY
	SALT AND PEPPER

Cream butter and work in other ingredients. Form butter into a roll, wrap in greaseproof paper and polythene and freeze. Cut off in slices when required to serve with grilled meat or fish.

BRANDY BUTTER

2 OUNCES BUTTER	2 TABLESPOONS BRANDY
2 OUNCES ICING SUGAR	

Cream butter and sugar and work in brandy. Pack into carton, pressing down well, cover, seal, label and freeze. To serve put into refrigerator 1 hour before serving time.

MELBA SAUCE

RASPBERRIES	SUGAR

Put raspberries in pan with very little water and heat very slowly until juice runs. Put through a sieve and sweeten to taste. Put into cartons, cover, seal, label and freeze. To serve, put into refrigerator 2 hours before serving time.

Chapter 16

PIES AND PIE FILLINGS

Pies are extremely useful for emergency meals when stored in the freezer. They are also a neat way of storing surplus fruit. Large pies are of course suitable for family meals, but there is great advantage in freezing individual fruit pies, turnovers, sausage rolls, meat patties and Cornish pasties ready for lunch-boxes and picnics.

Pastry frozen in bulk is not very satisfactory as it tends to crumble when rolled, and takes time to thaw. If it is required in this form, it is best stored in neat slabs like the commercial variety.

Short pastry and flaky pastry freeze equally satisfactorily either cooked or uncooked, but as with cake-making, all ingredients must be of the best. For good freezing, pastry should be made to a standard balanced recipe, rather than by a hit-and-miss method. Hot water crust pastry may be frozen when cooked, but is most usually combined with game or pork fillings. Since both of these present storage problems, its use is not really recommended unless hygienic conditions are perfect, and storage time is to be limited. Unbaked pastry will store up to 4 months, and baked pastry up to 6 months, but this must depend on the filling of pies, and as with all freezer items, it is wisest to arrange a short storage life and a quick turnover of food.

Pies and flans may be stored baked and unbaked. Almost all fillings are usable, except those with custard which separates. Meringue toppings are not advised as these toughen and dry during storage. Baked pies can be stored for a longer period, but the unbaked pie has a better flavour and scent and the pastry is crisper and flakier when baked from the freezer.

UNBAKED PASTRY

Unbaked pastry should be rolled, then formed into a square, wrapped in greaseproof paper, then in freezer paper or polythene, sealed and frozen. It should be thawed slowly, then cooked as fresh pastry. It is better to eat this pastry fresh-baked, and not to make pies for freezing again unbaked.

BAKED PASTRY

Baked pastry can most usefully be stored in the form of flan cases, patty cases and vol-au-vent cases. They should be baked in the usual way and cooled before freezing. For storage purposes, it is best to keep them in the cases in which they are baked, or in foil cases. Small cases may be packed in boxes in layers with paper between. To use, thaw at room temperature and fill. A hot filling may be used, and the cases heated in a low oven if wanted.

UNBAKED PIES

The pies may be prepared with or without a bottom crust. For fruit fillings, brush surface of bottom crust with egg white to prevent sogginess; for meat pies, brush crust with melted lard. Do not cut air vents in pastry before freezing. To prevent sogginess, it is better to freeze unbaked pies *before* wrapping them. Fruit pies may be made with cooked or uncooked filling. Apples tend to brown if stored in a pie for more than 4 weeks, even if treated with lemon juice, and it is better to combine frozen pastry and frozen apples to make a pie. Meat pies are best made with cooked filling and uncooked pastry (see Chapter 9 "Meat"). To bake, cut slits in top crust and bake unthawed as for fresh pies, allowing about 10 minutes longer than normal cooking time.

BAKED PIES

Cook pies in the normal way, cool quickly and freeze. A pie is best prepared and frozen in foil, but can be stored in a rust-proof and crack-proof container. The container should be put into freezer paper or polythene for freezing.

A cooked pie should be heated at 375°F. (Gas Mark 5) for 40–50 minutes for a double-crust pie, 30–50 minutes for a one-crust pie, depending on size. Pies may also be eaten thawed but not reheated, and small pies packed in lunch boxes at breakfast time will be ready for eating by mid-day.

FRESH FRUIT PIE FILLINGS

If time is short, it is convenient to freeze ready-made fruit pie fillings, ready to fit into fresh pastry when needed, and this is a good way of freezing surplus fruit in a handy form. Using the recipe method given here, try such combinations as rhubarb and orange, apricot and pineapple, or single fruits like cherries or blackberries. This mixture is best frozen in a spongecake tin or an ovenglass pie plate. A little cornflour or flaked tapioca will give a firm filling which cuts well and does not seep through the pastry.

RASPBERRY AND APPLE PIE

8 OUNCES THINLY SLICED COOKING APPLES
1 POUND RASPBERRIES
1 TABLESPOON LEMON JUICE
8 OUNCES SUGAR
2 TABLESPOONS TAPIOCA FLAKES
PINCH OF SALT

Mix all ingredients well in a bowl and leave to stand for 15 minutes. Line a pie plate with foil, leaving 6 inches rim. Put filling into foil, fold over, and freeze. Remove frozen filling from pie plate and store in freezer. Storage time: 6 months. To use, line pie plate with pastry, put in frozen filling, dot with butter, cover with pastry lid, make slits in top crust, and bake at 425°F. (Gas Mark 7) for 45 minutes.

Chapter 17

DAIRY PRODUCTS

The price of dairy products, particularly eggs, tends to fluctuate seasonally, and useful savings can be effected by freezing eggs, cream and cheese. There is an extra bonus in that top quality products are not always obtainable locally and may be purchased in bulk on special shopping trips, and that these dairy products are particularly useful for emergency entertaining.

MILK

There have been many recent developments in milk preservation, and today's "long life" and dried products fulfil most family needs for emergency supplies. However, it is possible to store pasteurised homogenised milk in the freezer (American experiments have shown that milk frozen at 0°F. can be held at this temperature for six months). For home use, milk can be frozen in cartons and stored for one month. 1 inch headspace should be allowed in containers, and the milk packaged in small enough quantities to be used at one time.

CREAM

Cream freezes very well if it contains 40% butterfat, as low butterfat cream tends to separate. Its storage life is 4 months, but when thawed it is most suitable for using with puddings or making into ice-cream. The texture can be heavy and grainy, which many people may not like for use with cereals or fruit; if used in hot coffee, its oil will rise to the surface. Cream for processing should be pasteurized and cooled rapidly, and packed in containers leaving 1 inch headspace. Devonshire and Cornish creams are heat-treated in preparation. 1 tablespoon sugar to each pint of cream will lengthen keeping time.

Those without home supplies of cream will find that

good quality high butterfat cream from shop or market will freeze perfectly in the carton in which it is purchased, without further treatment.

Cream should be thawed at room temperature, and light beating with a fork will restore smoothness.

Whipped cream may be frozen as a garnish for puddings, and is usefully prepared in anticipation of a party. Whip 1 pint cream with 1 ounce icing sugar until just stiff, and pipe rosettes on to foil covered cardboard. Freeze on floor of freezer for 2 hours. Working quickly, transfer to polythene bags and return to freezer. When wanted for use, put frozen garnish on to puddings and leave to stand 10 minutes at room temperature to thaw.

BUTTER AND MARGARINE
Both fats may be frozen in their original wrappings if still firm, or they may be over wrapped. Unsalted butter will keep for 6 months; salted butter for 3 months. When thawing, only take enough fat from the freezer to be used up within a week; thawing is best at room temperature overnight.

CHEESE
Most types of cheese can be frozen, but the most satisfactory are the hard types like Cheddar. Cheese should be frozen in small quantities, sufficient for one or two days' supply (i.e. 8 ounces or less) as it dries more quickly after having been frozen, and large cheeses should be divided and repackaged. Slices should be divided by double Cellophane before wrapping in foil or freezer paper. Storage life is 6 months.

Cream cheese does not freeze well and tends to fall apart on thawing. It can be frozen if blended with heavy cream for use later as a cocktail dip when it will be combined with mayonnaise and smoothness restored.

Cottage cheese made from pasteurized milk can be stored if frozen quickly to avoid water separation on thawing, and will keep for 4 months.

Special cheeses such as Camembert, Port Salut, Stilton,

Danish Blue and Roquefort may successfully be frozen, though the blue cheeses tend to crumble if cut while in the frozen state.

All cheeses must be very carefully wrapped and sealed to prevent drying-out and cross-contamination. They are best thawed in packaging in the refrigerator, but will take $1\frac{1}{2}$ to 2 hours at room temperature if required.

EGGS

Eggs can be stored perfectly in the freezer, and are very worthwhile, since their prices fluctuate seasonally. They should not be frozen in the shell as the shells may crack, the yolks tend to harden and will not beat smoothly into the whites. Whole eggs can be frozen, or quantities of yolks and whites separately. The addition of salt or sugar will prevent too much thickening.

Eggs to be frozen should be very fresh and of top quality. The eggs should be washed, and each one broken into a dish before processing to be examined for quality. Eggs may be packed in small or large containers according to their end-use. Small quantities may be frozen by the ice-cube method, individual cubes then being wrapped in foil, and a quantity of cubes put into polythene bags for storage. Re-usable waxed paper cups for freezing individual shelled eggs are also now obtainable (see Chapter 6 "Basic Equipment and Packaging Materials"). Very careful labelling is of course essential, particularly when salt or sugar have been added to be sure that these do not unbalance the recipe being used.

When eggs are packaged in quantity, it is as well to know their equivalent in liquid measure.

$2\frac{1}{2}$ tablespoons whole egg = 1 egg
$1\frac{1}{2}$ tablespoons egg white = 1 egg white
1 tablespoon egg yolk = 1 yolk

All eggs may be used as fresh eggs when they have been thawed, and can be stored for 8–10 months. They are best thawed unopened in a refrigerator, but for rapid use will take $1\frac{1}{2}$ hours unopened at room temperature.

In emergency, the container may be put into a bowl of cold water to speed thawing. Thawed eggs are best used at once, as quality deteriorates if they are left to stand, though egg whites will keep satisfactorily for 24 hours in a refrigerator after thawing.

Whole eggs

Break eggs individually, then put together in a bowl after examination. There should be no streaks of blood and the yolk should be well centred in the white. Blend the yolks and whites lightly with a fork to mix well but avoid getting a lot of air in. To avoid thickening, add $\frac{1}{2}$ teaspoon salt or $\frac{1}{2}$ tablespoon sugar to 5 eggs. Pack into cartons, carefully labelling if contents are sugared or salted (use sweet eggs for puddings, cakes and custards; salt eggs for scrambling, batters and omelettes).

Egg yolks

Egg yolks should be mixed very lightly with a fork so that they are not fluffy or lemon-coloured. They should be mixed with $\frac{1}{2}$ teaspoon salt to 6 yolks, or $\frac{1}{2}$ tablespoon sugar to 6 yolks.

Egg whites

Egg whites need no pre-freezing treatment. They should not be whisked but packed straight into cartons. They are excellent for meringues if used at room temperature.

Chapter 18

ICE CREAM

Bought or home-made ice cream may be stored in the
freezer for 4 months. If large containers of bought ice
cream are stored, and not repackaged into serving sizes
before storage, they should be used soon after opening.
When portions have been taken out of a large container,
a piece of foil over the unused portion will help to retain
flavour and texture.

Home-made ice cream for the freezer is best made with
pure cream and gelatine or egg yolks. For immediate
use, evaporated milk may be used, but the flavour is not
so good (before using, the unopened tin of milk should be
boiled for 10 minutes, cooled and left in a refrigerator
overnight).

A smooth commercial product cannot be produced
from a home freezer. The ingredients are different and
so is the equipment which gives a smooth ice cream.
Crank attachments can now be bought for freezers, which
work on the principle of the old dasher-churn, giving a
constant beating which produces smoothness. This is an
expensive luxury which will take time to repay itself,
and most cooks will make do with an electric whisk or a
liquidiser.

Ice cream should also be frozen quickly, or it will be
"grainy" and will keep this rough texture during long
storage. The correct emulsifying agent will help to give
smoothness. Egg, gelatine, cream or sugar syrup will
stop large ice crystals forming; gelatine gives a particularly smooth ice. Whipped egg whites give lightness.

Freezing diminishes sweetness, but too much sugar will
prevent freezing. The correct proportion is one part sugar
to four parts liquid.

BASIC METHOD
Whatever emulsifying agent is used, preparation is

similar. The mixture should be packed into trays and frozen until just solid about ½ inch from the edge. The mixture should be beaten quickly in a chilled bowl, then frozen for a further hour. This "freezing and beating" technique should be repeated for up to three hours. Some freezer owners save time by packing the ice cream into storage containers and freezing after the first beating, but results are not so smooth, and it is preferable to complete the ice cream before packing for storage.

BASIC FLAVOURINGS

Low temperatures affect flavourings, and these should be strong and pure (e.g. vanilla pod or sugar instead of essence; liqueurs rather than flavoured essences).

For *butterscotch*, cook the sugar in the recipe with 2 tablespoons butter until well browned, then add to hot milk or cream. For *caramel*, melt half the sugar in the recipe in a heavy saucepan over moderate heat, and add slowly to the hot milk. For *chocolate*, melt 2 ounces unsweetened cooking chocolate in 4 tablespoons hot water, stir until smooth, and add to hot milk. For *coffee*, scald 2 tablespoons ground coffee with milk or cream, and strain before adding to other ingredients. For *peppermint*, flavour with oil of peppermint and colour lightly green. For *praline*, make as caramel flavouring, adding 4 ounces blanched, toasted and finely-chopped almonds. For *eggnog*, stir several tablespoons rum, brandy or whisky into ice cream made with egg yolks. For *ginger*, add 2 tablespoons chopped preserved ginger and 3 tablespoons ginger syrup to basic mixture. For *maple*, use maple syrup in place of sugar and add 4 ounces chopped walnuts. For *pistachio* add 1 teaspoon almond essence and 2 ounces chopped pistachio nuts, and colour green.

To make ice creams with mixed flavours, try beating crushed fruit such as strawberries, raspberries or canned mandarin oranges into vanilla ice cream before packing into containers; swirl chocolate or butterscotch sauce through vanilla ice cream before packing; add chopped toasted nuts or crushed nut toffee to vanilla, coffee or chocolate ice cream; add a pinch of coffee powder to chocolate ice cream, or a pinch of chocolate powder to coffee ice.

To make moulds of ice cream, press the finished ice into metal moulds (if double-sided moulds are not available, use metal jelly moulds, cover tops with foil, wrap and seal). To turn out, invert mould on plate and cover metal with cloth wrung out in hot water. Two-flavoured moulds may be made by lining mould with one flavour and filling with another (chopped fruit or nuts may be added to the inner ice cream).

CUSTARD ICE

⅓ PINT MILK	2 OUNCES SUGAR
1 VANILLA POD	SMALL PINCH OF SALT
2 LARGE EGG YOLKS	⅓ PINT THICK CREAM

Scald milk with vanilla pod. Remove pod and pour milk on to egg yolks lightly beaten with sugar and salt. Cook mixture in a double boiler until it coats the back of a spoon. Cool and strain and stir in the cream. Pour into freezing trays and beat twice during a total freezing time of about 3 hours. Pack into containers, cover, seal and label, and return to storage in freezer.

GELATINE ICE

¾ PINT CREAMY MILK	3 OUNCES SUGAR
1 VANILLA POD	PINCH OF SALT
1 DESSERTSPOON GELATINE SOAKED IN 2 TABLESPOONS COLD WATER	

Heat ¼ pint milk with the vanilla pod to boiling point. Heat the soaked gelatine in a bowl standing in hot water, until the gelatine is syrupy. Pour warm milk on to gelatine, stir in sugar, salt and remaining milk. Remove vanilla pod and freeze mixture, beating twice during 3 hours total freezing time. Pack into containers, cover, seal, label and store in freezer. This mixture is particularly good for using with added flavourings such as chocolate or caramel.

115

CREAM ICE

| 1 PINT THIN CREAM | 3 OUNCES SUGAR |
| 1 VANILLA POD | PINCH OF SALT |

Scald cream with vanilla pod, stir in sugar and salt, and cool. Remove vanilla pod and freeze mixture to a mush. Beat well in a chilled bowl and continue freezing (about 2 hours total freezing time). Pack into containers, cover, seal and label, and store in freezer.

ORANGE SORBET

2 TEASPOONS GELATINE	1 TEASPOON GRATED ORANGE
½ PINT WATER	RIND
6 OUNCES SUGAR	½ PINT ORANGE JUICE
1 TEASPOON GRATED LEMON	4 TABLESPOONS LEMON JUICE
RIND	2 EGG WHITES

Soak gelatine in a little of the water and boil the rest of the water and sugar for 10 minutes to a syrup. Stir gelatine into syrup and cool. Add rinds and juices. Beat egg whites stiff but not dry, and fold into mixture. Freeze to a mush, beat once, then continue freezing allowing 3 hours total freezing time. This ice will not go completely hard. Pack into containers, cover, seal, label and store in freezer. For party occasions, this ice may be packed into fresh fruit containers. Scoop out oranges or lemons, wash them and fill with sorbet. Pack into containers, seal, label and store in freezer. If the ice has not been prepacked into fruit cases, the containers may be prepared before serving. To do this, scoop out oranges and lemons, wash and put into freezer wet so that they get a frosted surface. Thirty minutes before serving, scoop out the ice from its large container into the cases and leave in the freezer until serving time. The same recipe may be used for a lemon sorbet, using only lemon juice and rind instead of a mixture of orange and lemon.

FRESH FRUIT ICE

| ¾ PINT CREAM | 1½ TABLESPOONS CASTER SUGAR |
| ½ PINT FRUIT PUREE | |

Beat cream lightly until thick, stir in fruit puree and sugar, and pour into freezer tray and freeze without stirring. Put into containers, seal, label and store in freezer. This is particularly good made with fresh raspberries or with apricots poached in a little vanilla-flavoured syrup before sieving.

Chapter 19

BREAD, CAKES AND BISCUITS

It is a great advantage to store bread, cakes and biscuits in the freezer in both cooked and uncooked forms. They all freeze extremely well, and taste far better than the same items stored in tins. Bulk cooking, particularly with the aid of an electric mixer, can provide a supply of fresh-tasting cakes every day if really large batches are made and frozen. Home-baked bread becomes a practical pro-position when it is prepared in large quantities, and loaves from the freezer taste as fresh as the day they were baked. For school holidays, bags of scones and buns pro-vide filling picnics and packed meals, and large teas. Iced cakes can also be successfully stored, which saves a great deal of time for those who like to cook ahead for parties and special occasions, for these cakes cannot be stored well in a tin.

Small cakes, buns and rolls may most easily be frozen in polythene bags; small iced cakes are better packed in boxes. Large quantities of small iced cakes can be frozen in single layers, then packed in larger boxes with Cello-phane or greaseproof paper between layers. Bread and large cakes can both be frozen in polythene bags. While it is usually most convenient to pack cakes whole, some families may need meal-size wedges or individual pieces for lunch-boxes. These pieces may be frozen individually in bags or boxes, but it is easier to slice the whole cake in wedges before freezing, and withdraw slices as they are needed without thawing the whole cake.

When making cakes for freezing, it is most important to use good ingredients. Stale flour deteriorates quickly after freezing, so it is important to use fresh flour. Butter cakes retain a good flavour, but margarine is suitable for strongly flavoured cakes such as chocolate and gives a good light texture. Eggs should be fresh and well-beaten, as whites and yolks freeze at different speeds and will affect the texture of the cake. Icings for freezing are best made with butter and icing sugar; cakes should not be filled with boiled icing or with cream as these will crumble on thawing, as will icings made with egg whites. Fruit fillings and jams will make a cake soggy, and are best added after thawing. Flavourings must always be pure, as synthetics develop off-flavours in storage (this is particularly important with vanilla, and only pure extract or vanilla sugar made with a pod should be used).

If the freezer user is not an enthusiastic bread or cake cook, there is no reason why bought cakes should not be frozen for emergencies. Buns, Dundee cakes, unfilled sponges and sponge flan cases all freeze well and are very useful, but the same limitations concerning icings and fillings will apply to bought cakes as to home-baked ones. Crumpets and muffins are bought seasonal delicacies which can be frozen for future use.

UNCOOKED YEAST MIXTURES

It is possible to freeze unbaked bread and buns for up to 2 weeks, but proving after freezing takes a long time, and texture may be heavier. If unbaked dough is frozen, it should be allowed to prove once, and either shaped for baking or kept in bulk if storage in this form is easier. Brush the surface with a little olive oil or unsalted melted butter to prevent toughening of the crust, and add a little extra sugar to sweet mixtures. Single loaves or a quantity of dough can be packed in freezer paper or polythene, rolls can be packed in layers separated by Cellophane before wrapping in freezer paper or polythene. The dough should be thawed in a moist warm place, and greater speed will give a lighter textured loaf, then shaped and proved again before baking. Shaped bread and rolls should be proved at once in a warm place before baking.

COOKED YEAST MIXTURES

Cooked bread, rolls and buns freeze beautifully, and they freeze particularly well when one day old. Cooked bread and buns should be left to thaw in wrapping at room temperature; 1½ pound loaf takes about 3 hours. In emergency, bread may be thawed in a moderate oven, but will become stale very quickly.

SCONES
Baking powder scones may be frozen cooked or uncooked. Unbaked ones should only be stored for 2 weeks, otherwise they will keep for 2 months. There is no particular advantage in freezing unbaked scones. If they are ready-prepared, they can be baked in a hot oven without thawing, or partly thawed and then cooked.

PANCAKES AND GRIDDLECAKES
Pancakes, griddlecakes and drop scones freeze well, and are not only useful for tea time but for emergency savoury meals. They should be cooked as usual and cooled before packing. Large thin pancakes should be packed with a layer of Cellophane or greaseproof paper between each, stacked as a cake, then frozen in freezer paper or polythene. They can be easily separated while still frozen, or thawed in one piece in wrapping at room temperature, then wrapped wound filling and heated in a low oven or on a plate over steam, covered with a cloth. Griddlecakes and drop scones should be thawed in wrappings at room temperature before buttering.

WAFFLES
Waffles may be prepared in an iron and frozen, and reheated in an electric toaster or under a grill. Waffles were among the first frozen commercial products available in this country, but seem to be no longer obtainable.

SPONGECAKES
Basic sponge cakes are among the most useful frozen items. Fatless sponges can be stored for 10 months, but those made with fat store for about 4 months. Unbaked sponges will keep for 2 months, but are likely to lose volume in cooking. Prepare them in rustless baking tins

or foil if they are to be frozen unbaked. Delicate baked cakes may be frozen in paper or polythene, then packed in boxes to avoid crushing. Cake batter can be stored in cartons if this is easier for packing in the freezer; it should be thawed in the container before putting into baking tins, but if the mixture is allowed to thaw too long, the cake will be heavy. All baked cakes should be thawed in wrappings at room temperature, unless they are iced (see Icings and Fillings).

FRUIT CAKES

Rich fruit cakes may be stored in the freezer, but will keep very well in tins, so the tin method may be preferred if space is limited in the freezer. Dundee cakes, sultana cakes and other light fruit mixtures freeze very well. They should be defrosted in wrappings at room temperature.

SMALL CAKES

Small fruit cakes and sponge drops may be frozen in bags or boxes (layers should be divided by Cellophane or greaseproof paper). Cupcakes may be made in paper and foil cases, iced and frozen in single layers, then packed in boxes with paper between layers. Choux pastry and meringues can be frozen successfully, if unfilled, are best frozen in single layers, then packed in boxes because of their delicacy.

BISCUITS

Biscuits are the exception to the rule that the cooked frozen item is better than the uncooked one. Baked biscuits do freeze very well, but store equally well in tins, so there is no advantage in using valuable freezer space for them. The most useful and time-saving way of preparing biscuits is to freeze batches of any favourite recipe in cylinder shapes in freezer paper, polythene or foil. Overwrapping is advisable to avoid dents in the freezer from other packages. The dough will be all the better for having been frozen, giving light crisp biscuits. To use, leave in freezer wrapping in the refrigerator for 45 minutes until just beginning to soften, then cut in slices and bake; if the dough gets too soft it will be difficult to cut. Storage time: 2 months. If baked biscuits are to be stored, they must be carefully packed in layers in cartons with Cellophane or greaseproof paper between layers and with crumpled up paper in air spaces to safeguard freshness and stop breakages.

ICINGS AND FILLINGS

Cakes for storage should not be filled with cream, jam or fruit. Butter icings are best, but an iced cake must be absolutely firm before wrapping and freezing. Wrappings must be removed before thawing to allow moisture to escape and to avoid smudging icing. If sponge or flavoured cakes are to be packed for future icing, layers can be put together with Cellophane, foil or greaseproof paper between them, and they can be separated easily for filling when thawed.

FLAVOURINGS AND DECORATIONS

Flavourings must be pure for all icings and fillings, and vanilla extract or vanilla sugar should be used when this ingredient is necessary. Highly spiced foods may develop off-flavours, so spice cakes are best not frozen, though an ordinary gingerbread is perfectly satisfactory. Chocolate, coffee, and fruit-flavoured cakes freeze very well. There is no particular advantage in decorating cakes before they are frozen, and nuts, coloured balls, grated chocolate, etc. should be put on when the cake is fully thawed, just before serving; otherwise moisture may be absorbed and colour changes affect the appearance of the cake.

WHITE BREAD

2½ POUNDS PLAIN WHITE FLOUR

1 OUNCE FRESH YEAST

2 OUNCES FAT (BUTTER, MARGARINE OR LARD)

½ OUNCE SALT

1½ PINTS WARM WATER

Warm a large bowl and put in flour. Make a well in

centre and sprinkle salt round edge. Cream yeast with a little warm water and pour into the well. Add remaining water and warmed fat and mix well to a consistency like putty. Leave to prove until double its size. Divide into loaf tins and leave to prove again until bread reaches top of tins. Bake at 450°F. (Gas Mark 8) for 45 minutes, turning bread once in the oven. Cool on a rack and leave overnight in a tin before packing into bags and freezing. Thaw at room temperature for 2–3 hours.

CURRANT BREAD

1½ POUNDS WHITE FLOUR
4 OUNCES SUGAR
PINCH OF SALT
1 OUNCE FRESH YEAST
4 OUNCES WARM BUTTER

½ PINT WARM MILK
8 OUNCES MIXED DRIED FRUIT
2 OUNCES CHOPPED MIXED
  PEEL

Using a large warm bowl, mix flour, sugar and salt and add yeast creamed with a little sugar. Work in butter and milk, knead well and leave to prove for 1½ hours. Work in fruit and peel and put into loaf tins or shape into buns. Prove for 45 minutes. Bake at 375°F. (Gas Mark 5) for 45 minutes, turning loaves after 20 minutes. Small buns will only need to cook for 20 minutes. Cool on a wire tray, brushing with a mixture of milk and sugar to give a sticky finish. Store overnight in a tin and put into bags for freezing the next day.

CROISSANTS

1 OUNCE BUTTER
¼ PINT WARM MILK
1 HEAPED TEASPOON SALT
1½ TABLESPOONS SUGAR
1 OUNCE FRESH YEAST
  DISSOLVED IN A LITTLE
  WARM WATER

12 OUNCES PLAIN WHITE
  FLOUR
4 OUNCES BUTTER
1 EGG YOLK BEATEN WITH
  A LITTLE MILK

Put butter in bowl, pour on warm milk and add salt and sugar. Cool to lukewarm then add yeast and gradually add flour to give a soft dough. Cover bowl with dampcloth and leave for 2 hours. Knead dough, chill thoroughly, then roll into a rectangle. Spread butter lightly and evenly over dough. Fold over dough to a rectangle and roll again. Chill, roll and fold twice more at intervals of 30 minutes. Roll dough out to $\frac{1}{4}$ inch thickness and cut into 4 inch squares. Divide each square into 2 triangles, and roll each triangle up, starting at longest edge and rolling towards the point. Bend into crescent shapes, put on floured baking sheet, brush with beaten egg and milk and bake at 425°F. (Gas Mark 7) for 15 minutes. Cool, put into bags and freeze at once. These are nicest thawed at room temperature for 30 minutes, then lightly heated in the oven or under the grill.

BRIOCHE

8 OUNCES PLAIN FLOUR	6 OUNCES MELTED BUTTER
1 OUNCE YEAST	1 TEASPOON SALT
2 TABLESPOONS WARM WATER	1 TABLESPOON SUGAR
3 EGGS	

Put 2 ounces flour in a warm bowl and mix with yeast creamed with a little warm water. Put the little ball of dough into a bowl of warm water and it will expand and form a sponge. Put remaining flour into a bowl and beat in eggs thoroughly. Add butter, salt and sugar and continue beating. Add yeast sponge removed from water, and mix well. Cover with damp cloth and prove for 2 hours, then knead dough and leave in cool place overnight. Half-fill castle pudding tins with dough and prove 30 minutes. Bake at 450°F. (Gas Mark 8) for 15 minutes. Cool, put into bags and freeze. Thaw at room temperature for 45 minutes. Brioche may also be heated with the tops cut off and the centres filled with sweet or savoury mixtures (e.g. creamed mushrooms, chicken or shrimps).

BAPS

1 POUND PLAIN FLOUR	1 OUNCE YEAST
2 OUNCES LARD	$\frac{1}{2}$ PINT LUKEWARM MILK
2 LEVEL TEASPOONS SALT	AND WATER
1 TEASPOON SUGAR	

Sieve the flour and rub in lard and sugar. Cream the yeast in a little of the liquid and dissolve salt in the rest of the liquid. Mix into the flour, knead and prove until double in size. Divide into pieces and shape into small flat loaves about 4 inches across. Brush with milk, put on baking sheet, prove 45 minutes, then bake at 450°F. (Gas Mark 8) for 20 minutes. Cool, store until next day, put into bags and freeze. Thaw at room temperature for 45 minutes. Baps are useful freezer items to be used with hamburgers, or with a variety of fillings for lunchboxes.

GENOESE SPONGE CAKE

4 EGGS	3 OUNCES PLAIN FLOUR
4 OUNCES CASTER SUGAR	3 OUNCES MELTED BUTTER

Beat eggs and sugar over hot but not boiling water until light and thick. Melt butter gently, but do not make it hot. Take basin from heat and continue beating for 3 minutes, then fold in half the sifted flour and the melted butter very gently. Fold in remaining flour, put into a prepared 8 inch tin and bake at 400°F. (Gas Mark 6) for 45 minutes. This is a good cake for the freezer as it may be frozen as a round cake for use later with icing or fruit and cream; it may also be baked in a square tin and cut into pieces to make small fancy cakes which may be iced with butter icing before freezing.

VICTORIA SANDWICH

4 OUNCES MARGARINE	2 EGGS
4 OUNCES CASTER SUGAR	4 OUNCES SELF-RAISING FLOUR

Cream margarine and sugar until fluffy and almost white. Break in eggs one at a time and beat well. Fold in sifted flour and bake in two prepared 7 inch tins at 335°F. (Gas Mark 3) for 30 minutes. Leave in tin for 2 minutes, then cool. To freeze, put layers together with a double thickness of Cellophane or greaseproof paper between them, and put into polythene bag to freeze. These sponge layers may also be filled and iced with butter icing before freezing.

DUNDEE CAKE

8 OUNCES BUTTER
8 OUNCES CASTER SUGAR
5 EGGS
8 OUNCES SELF-RAISING FLOUR
½ TEASPOON NUTMEG
12 OUNCES MIXED CURRANTS
AND SULTANAS

3 OUNCES GROUND ALMONDS
3 OUNCES CHOPPED GLACE
CHERRIES
2 OUNCES CHOPPED CANDIED
PEEL
2 OUNCES SPLIT BLANCHED
ALMONDS

Cream butter and sugar until fluffy and add eggs one at a time with a sprinkling of flour to stop curdling. Beat well after adding each egg. Stir in flour, ground almonds, and the fruit lightly coated with a little of the flour. Put into buttered and lined 10 inch tin, smooth top, and arrange almonds on top. Bake at 325°F. (Gas Mark 3) for 2½ hours. Cool, pack into polythene bag and freeze.

ORANGE LOAF

2 OUNCES BUTTER
6 OUNCES CASTER SUGAR
1 EGG
GRATED RIND AND JUICE 1
SMALL ORANGE

2 TABLESPOONS MILK
7 OUNCES PLAIN FLOUR
2½ TEASPOONS BAKING
POWDER
½ TEASPOON SALT

Cream butter and sugar until fluffy and gradually add beaten egg with orange rind and juice, and milk. Add flour sieved with baking powder and salt, and fold into creamed mixture. Put into greased 2 pound loaf tin and bake at 375°F. (Gas Mark 5) for 1 hour. Cool, pack in polythene bag and freeze. To serve, thaw, slice and spread with butter.

GINGERBREAD

8 OUNCES GOLDEN SYRUP
2 OUNCES BUTTER
2 OUNCES SUGAR
1 EGG
8 OUNCES PLAIN FLOUR

1 TEASPOON GROUND GINGER
1 OUNCE CANDIED PEEL
1 TEASPOON BICARBONATE
OF SODA
MILK

Melt syrup over low heat with butter and sugar, and gradually add to the sieved flour and ginger, with the beaten egg. Mix soda with a little milk and beat into the mixture, and add chopped peel. Pour into rectangular tin and bake at 325°F. (Gas Mark 3) for 45 minutes. Cool, pack in polythene bag and freeze. As well as being a useful standby cake, gingerbread makes a delicious pudding served with apple purée and cream or ice cream.

CHOCOLATE CAKE

4 OUNCES MARGARINE	1 TABLESPOON COCOA
5 OUNCES CASTER SUGAR	2 EGGS
4 OUNCES SELF-RAISING FLOUR	1 TABLESPOON MILK

Slightly soften margarine, put all ingredients into bowl and blend until creamy and smooth. Bake in two 7 inch tins at 350°F. (Gas Mark 4) for 30 minutes. Cool and fill with *Chocolate Icing* made by blending together 6 ounces icing sugar, 1 ounce cocoa, 2 ounces soft butter and 2 dessertspoons hot water. Put icing on top. When cake is cold and icing firm, put into polythene bag and freeze. This is a particularly easy cake to make, and is beautifully moist and full of flavour even after some months in a freezer. With an electric mixer, it is easy to double or treble quantities for baking and freezing.

GOLDEN LEMON CAKE

1½ OUNCES BUTTER	6 OUNCES SELF-RAISING FLOUR
6 OUNCES CASTER SUGAR	¼ PINT MILK
3 EGG YOLKS	PINCH OF SALT
¼ TEASPOON LEMON ESSENCE	

Cream butter and sugar until fluffy and slowly add egg yolks and lemon essence. Add flour alternately with milk and the pinch of salt. Bake in two 8 inch tins lined with paper at 350°F. (Gas Mark 4) for 25 minutes. Cool, fill and ice with *Lemon Frosting* made by blending together 3 tablespoons butter, 1 tablespoon grated orange rind, 2 tablespoons lemon juice, 1 tablespoon water, 1 pound icing sugar. When cake is cold and icing firm, put into polythene bag and freeze. This is another cake which freezes very well and is beautifully soft and light after long storage.

CHOUX PASTRY

¼ PINT WATER	PINCH OF SALT
2 OUNCES LARD	2 SMALL EGGS
2¼ OUNCES FLOUR	

Bring water and lard to boil in pan and immediately put in flour and salt, draw pan from heat and beat until smooth with wooden spoon. Cook for 3 minutes, beating very thoroughly, cool slightly and beat in whisked eggs until the mixture is soft and firm but holds its shape. Pipe in finger lengths on baking sheet and bake at 425°F. (Gas Mark 7) for 30 minutes. For *Cream Puffs,* put mixture in small heaps, cover tin with a roasting tin or oven glass and bake at 425°F. (Gas Mark 7) for 1 hour. Cool and put into polythene bag to freeze. To serve, thaw, fill with whipped cream, and top with chocolate or coffee icing.

Chapter 20

PUDDINGS

Fresh and cooked fruits and purées, ice creams and various types of pie are obviously valuable when taken from the freezer for the pudding course of a meal, and all have long storage properties.

Sometimes, however, it is necessary to freeze different puddings in advance, perhaps for a party, or in quantity for holiday times. These puddings may include jellies and mousses, elaborate confections of butter creams and bread or cake crumbs, and even traditional steamed puddings. While recipes are open to individual experiment according to family needs, it is suggested these puddings should only be stored for a month at most, as their purpose is to provide menu variety quickly and there is little point in storing them longer.

Pudding and cake mixtures made to standard recipes may be steamed or baked, and are best in foil containers in which they can be steamed in their frozen state, then served with jam, custard or other sauce. It is better not to put jam or syrup in the bottom of these puddings before cooking, but dried fruit, fresh fruit or nuts may be added. Highly-spiced puddings may develop off-flavours quickly.

Jellies and mousses should also be made to standard recipes, and if space is no object in the freezer and many bowls are available they may be made in containers which will stand the freezer temperature and can be taken straight to table. They are best thawed in the refrigerator.

LEMON PUDDINGS

2 OUNCES CORNFLAKES	1 TABLESPOON GRATED LEMON PEEL
3 EGG WHITES	3 TABLESPOONS LEMON JUICE
4 OUNCES CASTER SUGAR	8 FLUID OUNCES DOUBLE CREAM
3 EGG YOLKS	

Crush cornflakes and sprinkle a little in each of six paper or foil jelly cases. Beat egg whites to soft peaks and gradually beat in sugar until stiff peaks form. In another bowl, beat yolks until thick and beat in lemon peel and juice until well mixed. Whip cream lightly, then fold egg yolk mixture and cream into egg whites until just mixed. Put mixture into cases, sprinkle with more corn-flake crumbs. Put a foil lid on each case, wrap in freezer paper or polythene and freeze. To serve, leave in foil cases in refrigerator for 30 minutes.

ICEBOX CAKE

6 OUNCES ICING SUGAR
4 OUNCES BUTTER
2 MEDIUM EGGS
2 TEASPOONS GRATED LEMON PEEL AND 2 TABLESPOONS LEMON JUICE *or* 2 TABLESPOONS COCOA AND 1 TEASPOON COFFEE ESSENCE
48 SPONGE FINGER BISCUITS

Cream icing sugar and butter together until light and fluffy and work in eggs one at a time. Gradually beat in peel and juice, or cocoa and coffee essence and beat hard until fluffy and smooth. Cover a piece of cardboard with foil and on it place 12 biscuits, curved side down. On this put one-third of creamed mixture. Put another layer of biscuits in opposite direction, more creamed mixture. Repeat layers, ending with biscuits. Cover completely with foil or freezer paper, seal and freeze. To serve, unwrap and leave in refrigerator for 3 hours. Cover completely with whipped cream (about ½ pint) and serve at once. Storage time: 1 month. This makes a large pudding giving 12 servings, and it may be pre-ferred in two packages.

ITALIAN COFFEE PUDDING

3 OUNCES CASTER SUGAR
4 OUNCES BUTTER
4 OUNCES FRESH WHITE BREADCRUMBS RUBBED FINE
5 TABLESPOONS STRONG BLACK COFFEE

Cream butter and sugar until light and fluffy. Work in

breadcrumbs and coffee until completely mixed. Press into foil dish, cover with foil lid and seal before freezing. To serve, remove lid and thaw in refrigerator for 45 minutes, cover with whipped cream and decorate with almonds or walnuts. Storage time: 1 month.

SWEDISH APPLECAKE

3 OUNCES BROWN BREADCRUMBS	2 TABLESPOONS BROWN SUGAR
1 OUNCE BUTTER	1 POUND PEELED COOKING APPLES

Gently fry breadcrumbs in butter until golden brown. Cook apples in very little water until soft and sweeten to taste. Sweeten breadcrumbs with brown sugar. Arrange alternate layers of crumbs and apples in buttered foil dish, beginning and ending with layers of crumbs. Press firmly into dish and leave to cool. Cover with a foil lid, seal and freeze. To serve, thaw without lid in refrigerator for 1 hour, turn out and serve with cream. Storage time: 1 month.

BAKED APPLE DUMPLINGS

8 APPLES	BUTTER
SUGAR	8 OUNCES SHORT PASTRY

Core apples, leaving $\frac{1}{4}$ inch core at bottom of each to hold filling. Fill with sugar and put a knob of butter in each. Put each apple on a square of pastry and seal joins. Bake at 425°F. (Gas Mark 7) for 25 minutes. Cool, pack into container or foil dish, cover, seal and freeze. To serve, heat at 375°F. (Gas Mark 5) while still frozen, for 20 minutes, and serve with cream, custard or hot apricot jam. Storage time: 1 month.

BERRY CREAM

1 POUND RASPBERRIES, CURRANTS, GOOSEBERRIES OR BLACKBERRIES	$\frac{3}{4}$ PINT WATER
	6 OUNCES SUGAR
	2 TABLESPOONS CORNFLOUR

Clean berries. Bring water to boil, add berries and sugar, and boil until fruit is soft. Mix cornflour with a little cold water, blend into hot liquid, and bring back to boil. Cool, put into containers, cover, seal and freeze. To serve, thaw in covered container in refrigerator for 1 hour, and serve with cream. Storage time: 1 month.

FRUIT MOUSSE

¼ PINT FRUIT PUREE	2 EGG WHITES
1 OUNCE CASTER SUGAR	JUICE OF ½ LEMON
¼ PINT DOUBLE CREAM	

Mix the fruit purée and sugar together. Lightly whip the cream, and whisk egg whites stiffly. Add lemon juice to fruit, then fold in cream and egg whites. If colour is pale, add a little food colouring. Put into foil container, cool, pack and freeze. To serve, thaw in refrigerator without lid for 2 hours. Storage time: 1 month.

Chapter 21

NO-COOK JAMS

An unusual way of using the freezer is to make un-cooked jams, which is useful for the cook with surplus fruit and little time for boiling and testing. These jams will keep for 6 months in the freezer, but should be packaged in small containers to be used in one serving. At the time of serving, if uncooked jams are stiff, or if "weeping" has occurred, stir them lightly to soften and blend. Colour and flavour will be like that of fresh fruit.

STRAWBERRY JAM

1½ POUNDS STRAWBERRIES
2 POUNDS CASTER SUGAR

4 FLUID OUNCES LIQUID
PECTIN

Mash or sieve strawberries and stir with sugar in a bowl. Leave for 20 minutes, stirring occasionally, then add pectin and stir for 3 minutes. Pour into small containers, cover tightly and seal. Leave at room temperature for 24–48 hours, until jelled. Store in freezer. Thaw 1 hour at room temperature.

RASPBERRY JAM

1½ POUNDS RASPBERRIES
3 POUNDS CASTER SUGAR

4 FLUID OUNCES LIQUID
PECTIN

Mash or sieve raspberries and stir with sugar. Leave for 20 minutes, stirring occasionally, then add pectin and stir for 3 minutes. Put into small containers, cover and seal. Leave for 24–48 hours until jelled. Store in freezer. Thaw 1 hour.

BLACKBERRY JAM

1½ POUNDS BLACKBERRIES
2¾ POUNDS CASTER SUGAR

4 FLUID OUNCES LIQUID
PECTIN

This jam is best made with large cultivated black-berries, as the small hard wild ones are difficult to mash without liquid and are rather "pippy". Mash berries and stir into sugar. Leave for 20 minutes, stirring occasionally, then add pectin and stir for 3 minutes. Put into small containers, cover and seal. Leave for 24–48 hours at room temperature until jelled. Store in freezer. Thaw 1 hour at room temperature.

APRICOT OR PEACH JAM

1½ POUNDS RIPE FRESH APRICOTS OR PEACHES

2 POUNDS CASTER SUGAR

4 FLUID OUNCES LIQUID PECTIN

1 TEASPOON POWDERED CITRIC ACID

Skin apricots or peaches and remove stones. Mash fruit and stir in citric acid and sugar. Leave for 20 minutes, stirring occasionally, then add pectin and stir for 3 minutes. Put into small containers, cover and seal. Leave for 24–48 hours at room temperature until jelled. Store in freezer. Thaw 1 hour at room temperature.

Chapter 22

PARTY FOODS

Most freezer owners know all about keeping special casseroles or puddings ready for unexpected guests and impromptu supper or lunch parties. Not so many, however, have realised the possibilities of keeping ready the makings of a small cocktail or buffet party ready for those guests who want more than a drink but less than a meal. Even for the large planned party, preparation and freezing ahead will be invaluable, for most cocktail "food" is fiddly and can use up a couple of days before a party in preparation time. Here are some of the most useful items:

Ice Cubes.
If space is available, freeze extra quantities and store in plastic bags (to keep cubes separate, wrap each in foil). For some drinks, such as large bowls of fruit punch, it is better to freeze large pieces of ice, using ice-trays without cube divisions; prepare a number of these and store in bags. For special drinks, freeze a sprig of mint, a twist of lemon or a cherry or strawberry into individual ice cubes.

Garnishes.
Freeze mint leaves in small packages for putting into fruit cups. Freeze parsley sprigs for decorating sandwiches or pies. Freeze strawberries with hulls on for garnishing fruit drinks or puddings (spread fruit on trays to freeze, then package).

SANDWICHES

Open sandwiches may be prepared and stored for 2 weeks (following the general rules for sandwich-making in Chapter 23). Ordinary sandwiches may be prepared up to 4 weeks ahead and left in large slices, then cut into small shapes for party serving. For special parties, rolled, ribbon or checkerboard sandwiches can be prepared but not sliced until after thawing. Open sandwiches are best arranged on a tray, baking sheet, or Cellophane-covered cardboard, without garnish, then wrapped, sealed and frozen.

CANAPES
Canapes can be made on thin slices of day-old bread, spreading to edge with butter and filling. They are best arranged on trays before packaging, and should be thawed for 1 hour.

PASTRY
Miniature pies and turnovers may be made and frozen unbaked. Bake them unthawed at 400°F. (Gas Mark 6) for 15–20 minutes and serve hot. Sausage rolls may be frozen unbaked, and baked unthawed at 400°F. (Gas Mark 6) for 20 minutes. Vol-au-vent cases may be frozen when baked, with fillings packaged separately, then thawed, filled and heated.

DIPS AND SPREADS
These are usually based on cream or cottage cheeses which freeze extremely well. Make as usual, omitting any salad dressing, mayonnaise, hard-cooked egg whites, or crisp vegetables. Thaw 5 hours at room temperature.

BACON WRAPS
Thin slices of streaky bacon without rinds may be wrapped round stuffed prunes, olives, chicken livers or cocktail sausages. Secure with toothpicks, freeze quickly on tray. Grill or cook in hot oven until bacon is crisp.

The following individual recipes are particularly good in the freezer.

COCKTAIL GRAPES
WHITE GRAPES	GRATED ONION
CREAM CHEESE	SALT
ROQUEFORT CHEESE	WORCESTER SAUCE

Split grapes and remove seeds. Blend equal parts cream cheese and Roquefort and season highly with grated onion, salt and Worcester sauce. Stuff grapes with filling, place on small trays, package and freeze. These should be frozen for no longer than 2 weeks. Thaw at room temperature for 1 hour before serving.

CREAM CHEESE BALLS

CREAM CHEESE
WALNUTS OR ONIONS
SALT AND PEPPER

CHOPPED NUTS OR CRUSHED
CRISPS

Mash cream cheese with finely chopped walnuts or onions, and season well with salt and pepper. Roll balls about ¾ inch diameter, and roll in chopped nuts or crushed crisps. Arrange on trays, wrap and freeze. Thaw for 1 hour at room temperature and serve on cocktail sticks.

BLUE CHEESE BUTTER

8 OUNCES DANISH BLUE
  CHEESE
4 OUNCES SOFT BUTTER
2 TABLESPOONS PORT

2 TABLESPOONS CHOPPED
  PARSLEY
½ MINCED OR GRATED
  ONION

Blend together all ingredients with a fork (this will be easier if the bowl is placed over a pan of hot water). Pack into container, chill and freeze. Thaw in refrigerator until of spreading consistency and use on small salted biscuits or on oatcakes.

CREAM CHEESE AND LIVER PATE

1 POUND CREAM CHEESE
8 OUNCES LIVER SAUSAGE

WORCESTER SAUCE
SALT AND PEPPER

Blend together cream cheese and liver sausage until smooth and season well with Worcester sauce, salt and pepper. Pack into container and freeze. Thaw in refrigerator until just soft, and serve as paté with toast, as a canape spread, or as a sandwich filling.

Chapter 23

SANDWICHES AND PACKED MEALS

All types of bread freeze well, so logically the freezing of sandwiches is an important aid to anyone catering for a busy family. Sandwiches may be prepared for individual meals, for parties or meetings, and for packed lunches.

Each filling has a different keeping time, but the best general rule is to store sandwiches in the freezer for no longer than 4 weeks. Sandwiches should be packaged in groups of six or eight rather than individually, and an extra slice or crust of bread at each end of the package will help to prevent drying-out.

Avoid fillings which contain cooked egg whites, which become dry and tough with freezing; *also avoid* raw vegetables in fillings such as celery, lettuce, tomatoes and carrots; *also avoid* salad cream or mayonnaise which will curdle and separate when frozen and soak into the bread when thawed. To prevent fillings seeping through, butter the bread liberally, which will be easier if the bread is day-old.

Have plenty of variety in sandwiches by using a number of breads. Whole wheat, rye, pumpernickel and fruit breads are all excellent (the brown breads are particularly good for fish fillings, and the fruit bread for cheese and sweet fillings).

Sandwiches should not be frozen against the freezer wall as most items are, as this will result in uneven thawing. Put the packages a few inches from the wall of the freezer, and see the edges of the sandwiches are towards the wall. Sandwiches should be defrosted in their wrapping at room temperature for four hours.

When quantities of sandwiches are to be prepared, an assembly-line technique will speed up matters. Try doing them this way:

1. Soften butter or margarine (but do not melt).

2. Prepare fillings and refrigerate ready for use.

3. Assemble wrapping materials.

4. Assemble breads and cut (or split rolls or baps).

5. Spread bread slices, going right to the edge to prevent fillings soaking in.

6. Spread fillings evenly on bread to ensure even thawing time.

7. Close and stack sandwiches.

8. Cut with a sharp knife (sandwiches are best left in rather large portions, such as half-slices) and leave crusts on.

9. Wrap sandwiches tightly in Cellophane, then in foil or other moisture-vapour-proof wrap. With an inner wrapping, the other covering may be removed and retained at home and the neat inner package taken in a lunch box for thawing.

10. Label and freeze.

The following fillings are all very satisfactory:

CHEESE
Cream cheese with olives and peanuts
Cream cheese with chutney
Cream cheese with chopped dates, figs or prunes
Cottage cheese with orange marmalade or apricot jam
Blue cheese with roast beef
Blue cheese with chopped cooked bacon
Cheddar cheese and chopped olives or chutney

FISH
Mashed sardines, hard-boiled egg yolk and a squeeze of lemon juice
Minced shrimps, crab or lobster with cream cheese and lemon juice
Tuna with chutney
Canned salmon with cream cheese and lemon juice

MEAT AND POULTRY

Sliced meat such as tongue, corned beef, luncheon meat and chutney

Sliced roast beef with horseradish sauce

Sliced roast lamb with mint jelly

Sliced chicken or turkey with ham and chutney

Minced ham with chopped pickled cucumber and cream cheese

For filling individual lunch boxes, sandwiches may be frozen individually, and can be boxed and stored with other items, labelled carefully, so that the owner may withdraw his lunch box from the freezer without rummaging among all the contents. This can be a great boon if families have to be left on their own since all guesswork is eliminated, individual tastes catered for, and time saved when people are leaving at different hours of the morning.

In addition to sandwiches for lunch boxes, cakes may be included. These can be single small cakes or larger cakes which have been cut into portions and frozen separately. Pies may also be wrapped and frozen in single-serving wedges. Small meat or chicken patties can be used, or items such as fried chicken legs. To save time in assembling the lunch box, home-made biscuits can also be frozen in small quantities for each box. Individual boxes of sugared raspberries or strawberries, fruit salad in syrup, sweetened apple puree, fruit juices or tomato juice can also be included. Soups can be packaged in small containers to be eaten cold or heated if possible.

Chapter 24

COMPLETE MEALS FROM THE FREEZER

It is a rare occasion when a freezer-owner needs to produce a complete meal from stored items, including appetiser, main course, vegetables and pudding, since menu-planning is obviously governed by current availability of fresh foods and ruling prices.

Bad weather, however, may force the cook back on stored food. Families may have to be left without the chief menu-planner and cook available, or a party meal for a number of people must be prepared at short notice when shops are shut.

In all these cases, a freezer which contains not only the basic fresh foods, but also a number of pre-cooked items will be invaluable. A lot of people would like to prepare "dinner-on-a-tray" type meals for just these occasions, such as are available commercially, but this is not practical in the average kitchen. These commercial meals are carefully and scientifically planned so that with the same oven heat the meat and vegetables will be warmed through in the time it takes to bake pastry and roast potatoes. Home planners must instead prepare individual items which can be used together and if possible have the same thawing or heating times.

The best plan for emergencies is to be sure that there are always soups, juices or pates for appetiser courses or light snacks; casseroles and/or meat pies and/or cold meats for main courses; fish for variety; potatoes, spaghetti or rice for bulk; vegetables and fruit for colour and sharp flavours; puddings or ices to add zest to a meal. If it is possible to label each cooked item with the method of thawing and/or heating, an emergency can be coped with by even an inexperienced member of the family. If a whole series of ready meals is likely to be wanted, as in school holidays, a list of menus can be pinned up, and the suggested main courses, vegetables and puddings attached to each other for speedy identification.

Individual lunch boxes or teas can be prepared, even with single-size portions all packed ready in one container. Only trial and error will provide the answers for this type of menu-making in individual households, but there is one useful rule to observe: aim at a one-month freezer life and a rapid turnover for prepared meals. Here are some ideas for complete meals from suggestions and recipes in the preceding chapters.

LUNCHEON MENU
Tomato Juice
Spaghetti with Meat Balls
Individual Lemon Puddings

SUMMER LUNCH
Clear Chicken Soup
Beef Galantine and Cucumber Salad
Fresh Fruit Ice

WINTER LUNCH
Grapefruit in Syrup
Jugged Hare, French Beans and Potatoes in Jackets
Raspberry and Apple Pie with Cream

SCHOOL HOLIDAY LUNCH
Tomato Soup
Meat Loaf, Peas and Chips
Baked Apple Dumplings

WINTER DINNER PARTY
Chicken Liver Pate
Beef in Wine, Sweet Corn Kernels and Mashed Potatoes
Lemon Icebox Cake

SUMMER DINNER PARTY
Potted Shrimps

Roast Chicken, Bread Sauce, Mixed Vegetables and
   New Potatoes
Orange Sorbet

CHILDREN'S TEA PARTY
Sardine Sandwiches
Sausage Rolls
Chocolate Cake
Meringues with Cream

LUNCH BOX
Tomato Soup (hot or cold)
Cornish Pasties
Gingerbread

Chapter 25

FREEZING AND USING LEFTOVERS

While the idea of leftover food is always unattractive, circumstances often occur when the amount of food cooked is just too much, but the freezer can accommodate these remains to be turned into useful meals at a not-too-distant date. Leftovers should not be stored for longer than 2 weeks, and must be frozen quickly.

VEGETABLES
Cooked vegetables do not freeze satisfactorily. If they are not likely to be used the next day and can be kept in the refrigerator, puree them with a little stock and freeze by the ice-cube method (see Chapter 7 "How to Pack for Freezing)." Use these cubes of puree as a basis for soups, stews or sauces.

FRUIT
Leftover fruit is likely to be eaten quickly and is best stored in the refrigerator.

SOUP
Small quantities of soup can be frozen for individual servings or to use as a sauce for meat or fish, or to use in a pie (see Chapter 15 "Soups and Sauces").

SAUCES
Sauces can be frozen in individual portions by the ice-cube method (see Chapter 7 "How to Pack for Freezing") to be used with meat, fish, vegetables or pasta. Italian tomato paste, a useful sauce base, is often leftover in its tin or tube, and can also be frozen by the ice-cube method.

CAKES AND PIES
These can be frozen in individual slices for use in lunch boxes or at picnics.

EGGS
Leftover yolks and whites can be frozen individually or in quantity (see Chapter 17 "Dairy Products"). When thawed, these may be used exactly as fresh eggs.

COFFEE AND TEA
This may sound odd, but frozen cubes of coffee and tea are invaluable in the summer for iced coffee and iced tea, since ordinary ice cubes weaken the drinks. Wrap cubes in foil and package in bags.

BREADCRUMBS
It is often difficult to gauge quantities when preparing ordinary or buttered crumbs. Freeze the unused crumbs in bags for quickly garnishing dishes which are finished off under a grill or in the oven. Bread slices can be frozen and grated into crumbs while still hard for use as garnish or in stuffings.

MEAT AND POULTRY
Slices of cooked meat and poultry may be frozen on their own, packing them compactly. They may also be frozen in gravy or sauce. Poultry stuffing should be removed and frozen separately. For some households it may be more practical to cube or mince the leftover meat for freezing, ready to use with sauces for serving with rice or spaghetti, or to use in recipes which require cooked meat. It is better still to prepare the meat immediately as a meat loaf, rissoles or a casserole and freeze in this form if this is the possible end-use, as this will save subsequent thawing and preparation time. Small quantities of poultry or ham may be turned into pastes or spreads to be used subsequently for sandwiches or toast (avoid mayonnaise or sandwich spread in their preparation which will curdle and separate on thawing).

FISH

This is best flaked and made into a spread to freeze for sandwiches or toast. Cooked fish is not worth freezing in any other form; since it is spoiled by overcooking, and the time taken to reheat the dish is as long as the original cooking time. Some housewives may want to make fish-cakes and freeze these, and a recipe is included in Chapter 12 "Fish and Shellfish".

Chapter 26

STORING AND USING BOUGHT FROZEN FOOD

A range of commercially frozen foods can usefully be stored in the home freezer. Such items as orange juice are costly to produce in this country from fresh fruit while the commercially frozen cans are small, neat and easily stored and represent good value. Vegetables and fruit are of course worth buying ready-frozen if there is insufficient home produce, and certain confectionery items such as eclairs, cream sponges and ice cream are useful in a household where there is little time for baking. Pastry is another valuable freezer item, and the commercially frozen kinds are cheap and failure-proof for the inexperienced cook.

Correct handling of commercially frozen foods is just as important as the handling of those which are home frozen. The greatest problem is allowing the packages to begin thawing before they are stored at home, and it is important to cut down the time between purchase and storage. This can best be done by buying frozen items as the last purchase on the shopping list, rather than leaving them in a warm car. Boxes and cartons will retain their chill if insulated by other shopping in the centre of a box or basket. Ideally, they should be put into an insulated bag, or wrapped in several layers of newspaper.

As soon as the packages reach home, they should be put into the freezer and not left around in the kitchen. A slight raising of temperature before storing can result in loss of colour and flavour.

As with home-frozen food, rotate commercial purchases on a first-in-first-out basis. Put new purchases at the back or bottom of the freezer, and use first those which have been stored longest. To make this easier, it is best to label packages as bought.

Instructions for thawing and using frozen products are given in detail on each package and should be strictly adhered to.

The housewife who has the problem of leaving complete freezer meals in her absence (see Chapter 24 "Menus for Complete Freezer Meals") may find it easier to do so with the help of commercial products since the cooking instructions may be more easily followed by inexperienced cooks than those on her home-frozen meals. Commercial packs can be put together in large bags and clearly labelled for each day's use. Useful items for such meals are Braised Beef Slices, Chicken and Mushroom Casserole, Steaklets and Beefburgers, Chicken Pie or Steak and Kidney Pie, supported by a variety of frozen vegetables and chips. Raspberries, strawberries, eclairs, mousses or sponges filled with cream can complete the menu.

It is often useful to know the weight of commercially frozen packs comparable to market-bought items:

FISH	*Weight of frozen fish*	*Comparable weight of market-bought fish*
COD	13 OUNCES	1 POUND 12 OUNCES
HADDOCK	13 OUNCES	1 POUND 12 OUNCES
PLAICE	13 OUNCES	1 POUND 10 OUNCES
KIPPERS	7½ OUNCES	1 POUND 7 OUNCES

FRUIT JUICE	*Weight of frozen juice*	*Equivalent in fresh fruit*
ORANGE	6 FLUID OUNCES	JUICE OF 12 ORANGES
GRAPEFRUIT	6¼ FLUID OUNCES	JUICE OF 6–8 GRAPEFRUIT

VEGETABLES	*Weight of frozen vegetables*	*Comparable weight of market-bought vegetables*
PEAS	10 OUNCES	1 POUND 12 OUNCES
BROAD BEANS	10 OUNCES	2½ POUNDS
BRUSSELS SPROUTS	10 OUNCES	1 POUND
SLICED GREEN BEANS	9 OUNCES	1 POUND
SPINACH	12 OUNCES	1½ POUNDS

Chapter 27

BUYING IN BULK

Buying in bulk saves not only money but time for the freezer owner. Catering packs can bring prices down by one-third, together with the extra saving on fares or petrol involved in small shopping expeditions, and can also save a lot of time in the kitchen.

Not all freezer owners have large gardens or farms, so the greater part of their food must in any case be bought; likewise not all freezer owners are necessarily superb cooks, and are happier buying their sausage rolls or fishcakes. Where children are concerned, large quantities of chips, peas, fish fingers and ice-cream may be their staple diet, and all these items can be bought in bulk.

The housewife on good terms with her grocer or greengrocer can ask for catering packs prepared by commercial firms, which are willingly supplied by the manufacturers, though it is only fair to give a minimum order of about £4 for these at one time. Main items supplied like this are peas, sprouts and chips, raspberries and strawberries. If a local shop is unwilling to negotiate, manufacturers will often supply direct from their local depot, given a decent minimum order. Also from local shops, by negotiation, come half-gallon drums of ice-cream, invaluable for school holidays and parties. Even small village shops now sell family economy packs of the more popular fruit and vegetables, usually in 1 pound or 1½ pound sizes, which are all the owner of a small freezer may be able to accommodate, but these will still give a useful saving over the tiny packs.

Opinions are divided on the value of buying meat in bulk. It is possible to buy whole or half animals from a local butcher and have these jointed, but since each animal only has a limited number of shoulders and legs, it can involve the customer in a number of the cheaper cuts and offal which she may not be happy to give room to in her freezer. A better buy can be the more expensive cuts, carefully prepared, from a lamb or beef specialist, which can be used for special-occasion meals; an alternative is to buy the very cheap imported legs of lamb, or shoulders, in season, transferred quickly from the butcher's freezing room to the home freezer.

Apart from local suppliers, the following organisations have proved their worth in supplying bulk orders to the individual customer.

W. BROOKS & SON, 40–50 HATCHAM ROAD, LONDON, S.E.15. Delivers in Greater London and some parts of the Home Counties, with a minimum order of £3, cash on delivery. Catering packs include vegetables, fruit, poultry, meat, fish and shellfish, and bakery items. There are basic items like fish fingers, sausage rolls and hamburgers, luxuries like scampi and salmon, and special "home-made" food like pate and fresh fruit salad.

SINNETS DISTRIBUTORS LTD., ADELAIDE STREET, MACCLESFIELD, CHESHIRE (*Macclesfield* 6341) and ENOCH STREET, MANCHESTER, 10 (*Collyhurst* 4511). Meat, poultry, fish, vegetables, fruit, ice cream and bakery items delivered within 50 miles of Manchester for £10 minimum order. No minimum order charge if customer collects order.

TURNER FOODS (OVERSEAS) LTD., STATION WAY, BUCKHURST HILL, ESSEX (504–5201). Catering packs delivered within 10 miles of Buckhurst Hill.

WINCHESTER FROZEN FOODS, BAR END, WINCHESTER, HANTS. (*Winchester* 62207). Delivery of frozen foods within 40 miles of Winchester.

ASHFORD CREAMERIES LTD., BOWLING GREEN ROAD, STOURBRIDGE, WORCS. (*Stourbridge* 4747). Frozen foods supplied in Birmingham and West Midlands.

W. E. DRYDEN, 16 ALLAN STREET, DUNDEE (*ODU* 2 22952). Weekly deliveries of frozen food within 40 miles of Dundee.

S. HILBERT LTD., GOODS YARD, DORKING NORTH,

Dorking, Surrey. (*Dorking* 2810). Frozen foods supplied within 15 miles of Dorking.

Hertfordshire Frozen Foods Ltd., Wiggen Hall Road, Watford, herts. (*Watford* 20396). All frozen foods delivered within 25 mile radius of Watford.

Freezer and Food Ltd., Deepfreeze Centre, High Street, Chobham, Surrey (*Chobham* 8004). Specially prepared meat and poultry and a wide range of commercial frozen foods.

Gibson Refrigeration Ltd., 10 Trafalgar Road, Horsham, Sussex (*Horsham* 5328). Fruit, vegetables, fish, ice cream and meat products, which must be collected from Horsham by customers.

Fine Foods (Explorator) Ltd., Riverside Road, Lowestoft, Suffolk (*Lowestoft* 2980). Fish of all kinds, including fish fingers, shellfish, and also poultry and ice cream. Minimum order £7 for delivery north of the Broads.

M.K.G. Food Products Ltd., Westgate, Aldridge, Staffs (*Aldridge* 53131) and Old Coach Road, Bilborough, Nottingham (*Nottingham* 292306). Fish, meat, fruit, vegetables, ice cream with deliveries within 30 miles of Birmingham and Nottingham.

Surrey Frozen Foods Ltd., 69 Broadway, Stoneleigh, Surrey (*Ewell* 0275). All frozen foods delivered in Surrey, or may be collected by customers.

Lord Fisher, Kilverstone, near Thetford, Norfolk (*Thetford* 2263). From here come Norfolk "hoggets" or young lambs. The meat may be ordered in individual joints or in sides ready jointed, consisting of leg, loin and shoulder. The meat has a beautiful flavour and tenderness, and the cost is £6.0.0d for a side weighing about 19 pounds. Carriage and packing is included, and despatch is every Wednesday.

Merry Monarch, 6–7 West Smithfield, London, E.C.1. (01 236 9236). This firm specialises in beef of top quality, trimmed and ready to freeze. Veal is also supplied, and mixed barbecue packs of poultry, lamb and pork. Meat is delivered by express post or passenger train, and there are weekly deliveries in Kent, Sussex, Berks, Wilts, Glos., Oxon, London and London suburbs.

HARRODS, KNIGHTSBRIDGE, LONDON, S.W.1. (01 730 1234). Deliveries in the usual store delivery area, or by rail at the customer's expense, of vegetables, fruit, poultry and meat. Example of their bulk items is a dozen corn cobs costing 1/– each, or two dozen chicken quarters for 50/–. The store specialises in beautifully prepared meat, and frequently makes offers to freezer users of bulk quantities of chops or steaks, making a good saving on top quality meat. All meat is cut to weight in quantities requested, packed in polythene, sealed and labelled for easy recognition.

BRAKE BROS. (POULTRY PACKERS) LTD., LENHAM HEATH, MAIDSTONE, KENT. (*Lenham* 484).

Cooked, frozen and fresh poultry, meat, seafood, vegetables, sausages, pastry, fruit, ice-cream. Deliveries in Kent and parts of Surrey and Sussex.

One word of warning about bulk packages of fruit and vegetables. If it is planned to use only part of a bulk pack at one time, it is better to repack items in a smaller quantity before they go into the freezer, rather than leaving larger packages half-used, or having to repack after using a small amount. If it is planned to repack, buy items which are dry-packed so that vegetables can be quickly shaken out in quantities required rather than chopped or sawn apart.

INDEX

Recipe Index

General Index

155

DEEP FREEZING
MENUS & RECIPES
Mary Norwak

The techniques of deep freezing have already caused a revolution in the kitchen. The owner of the deep freeze can plan her menus for several weeks or even months ahead, and need no longer fear the arrival of unexpected guests, or the chore of shopping several times a week.

This book is a sequel to Mary Norwak's earlier success, *A Complete Guide to Deep Freezing*, which provided the basic information on freezing, packaging and storing. *Deep Freezing Menus and Recipes* includes over 200 further recipes on all types of dishes from fish, meat and poultry to pastry, puddings, cakes and breads.

The author has also added a comprehensive table of storage times and a special chapter on how to pack cooked dishes.

THE I HATE TO COOKBOOK
Peg Bracken

"This little gem of a book ... Her style is as delicious as her recipes."

Jean Kerr

If, like Peg Bracken, you hate to cook, this book tells you all about the easiest ways with vegetables, salads and dressings, last-minute meals, pot-luck suppers and lunches, children's parties and dinners to impress people. Even if you quite like cooking, you'll find plenty of new and exciting recipes in
The I Hate to Cookbook